ISLAM
REDISCOVERED

*Discovering Islam
from its Original Sources*

Maulana Wahiduddin Khan

Goodword
B·O·O·K·S

First published in 2001
Reprinted 2002
© Goodword Books 2002

GOODWORD BOOKS
1, Nizamuddin West Market
New Delhi 110 013
Tel. 435 5454, 435 6666, 435 1128
Fax 435 7333, 435 7980
E-mail: info@goodwordbooks.com

Contents

※❀❀❀※

Preface

The theme of this book is evident from its title: *Islam Rediscovered: Discovering Islam from its Original Sources*. Its purpose is to present Islam as it is, drawing on its original sources rather than judging it by the later day interpretations and commentaries or the practices of present day Muslims in different parts of the world. A distinction is made between Islam as presented by the Prophet Muhammad ﷺ and his companions (information about which is available to us in the Qur'an and the *sunnah*) and Islam as represented by later Muslim generations — both in theory and practice. This is what we call the scientific approach.

We are living in the age of the media. Before the advent of the modern media there were large numbers of people in the world who knew nothing of Islam. With the invention of the printing press and now the electronic media it is difficult to find today a single person who is unaware of it.

But there is a clear-cut difference. In previous ages it happened that wherever Islam spread people were so impressed with it that most of them accepted it as their religion. That is why today we find more than one billion

Muslims throughout the world. Strangely enough the present day publicity given to Islam has produced only a negative effect. People are now generally allergic to Islam rather than being interested in it.

In previous centuries when Islam was introduced, people used to say: Yes "Mr Islam welcome to you." Now when Islam is presented to them they say: "No thank you." Why is there this difference? The answer is very simple. In previous centuries Islam was introduced to the people of the world through its scriptures, as it is — without the slightest change in its original message. Whereas in modern times, Islam is being introduced through the negative practices of certain Muslims as reported by the media.

There is a further and more severe problem that of selective reporting. According to their own criteria the media is interested only in 'hot' news, although so much 'soft' news is available about the Muslim people. Because of their ingrained professionalism, they do not allow this 'soft' news to find its way into their columns of their broadcasts.

Islam is the religion of nature. If it were to be presented in its original form, people would turn to it quite naturally, for example, when a recently converted American by the name of Gary Miller was asked why he had converted to Islam, he replied: "I didn't convert to Islam I have rather reverted to my original religion."

Unfortunately, a section of Muslims is engaged in violent and aggressive activities, wrongfully indeed, in the name of Islam. It is such news as, through the media, has a great impact upon the general public and creates serious misunderstandings. People have come to take Islam as a militant religion. Since modern man is in search of peace, he finds no appeal in a religion which, as presented by the media, is one of hatred and violence.

This book attempts to introduce Islam as it is. It calls for a distinction to be made between Islam and the practices of Muslims. Taking a scientific attitude, you have to see Islam in the light of the Islamic scriptures and not judge it by Muslim conduct.

For surely, if you want to know what democracy is, you will examine the ideology of democracy as established by its champions. You will not form an opinion about the democratic system merely on the basis of observing some self-styled democratic nation. Everyone who wants to know what Islam is, should follow this scientific method while trying to form his opinion on Islam.

We are living in an age of information. This is the age of the knowledge explosion. Today, everyone wants to know more and more about everything, including religion. The result is that, on the subject of religion, people are far better informed than ever before. But there is a difference. About other religions, people generally know what is enshrined in their religious books. Whereas the case of Islam is the opposite. Their information about Islam is derived from unauthentic sources. The reason for this lies with the Muslims and not with anyone else. The Muslims of modern times are engaged in violence everywhere in the name of Islam. Violence, however, is not limited only to Muslims. It is found in every community and in every group. But there is a basic difference between the two. When the adherents of other religions engage in violence, they do not do so in the name of their religion. But the violence engaged in by the Muslims is being done in the name of Islam.

These violent activities of the Muslims reach the people through the media. As modern media is a "hot news"-based industry, these violent events are flashed in the media. For this reason, people come to regard Islam as a religion of violence. It is only among Muslims that all violent activities are carried out in the name of religion.

In practice, only a tiny minority of Muslims is engaged in such violent activities. However, since other Muslims neither condemn these activities, nor disown them outright, it is but natural for people to attribute their violent propensities to their religion. But the scientific way of study is to distinguish Islam from the deeds of Muslims, just as the ideology of democracy is studied by distinguishing it from the acts of democratic countries.

The aim of this book is to present Islam as it is enshrined in its sacred scriptures, so that it may be brought before the people in its true form. The authentic source of information about Islam is the Qur'an. The Qur'an, according to Muslim belief, was revealed by God to the Arabian Prophet Muhammad, may peace be upon him. The second source of knowledge about Islam is the *sunnah*, i.e., the words, deeds and sanctions of the Prophet Muhammad ﷺ. The lives of the companions of the Prophet provide another later source. Then, there is a full stop in this matter. No other person or historical record enjoys the status of source of Islam.

However, this book does not claim to be a comprehensive introduction to Islam. That is something which can be had only by studying Islam directly through its basic scriptures, that is, the Qur'an and Sunnah. This book thus presents a fundamental introduction for those who want to understand Islam as it is. Its aim is to provide a proper background in the light of which the original sources of Islam may be studied.

I hope that this book will be useful for those who want to know about the original Islam, as opposed to the "religion" represented by certain self-styled Muslim leaders introduced to us by the media.

Finally, I would like to thank Anna Khanna, Farida Khanam, Rashdan M. Radzi, Alaref Ahmad, and Maulana Anis Luqman Nadvi for their immense help in making this book possible.

Manchester, U.K.   Wahiduddin Khan
June 23, 1999

1

❀❀❀

Search for Truth

Man is a born seeker — a veritable truth-seeking animal. Every human being regards himself as incomplete until he has found that supreme principle by which he can explain his existence in this world and discover the purpose and meaning of his life.

Everyone is a seeker. True. But few are finders. Why? Because, where seeking is instinctive, finding is the outcome of one's own conscious effort.

In the pre-Islamic period, there were certain individuals in Arabia, called *Hunafa*. They were all truth seekers. Confining themselves to solitary places, they would remember God and say: "O God if we had known how to worship You, we would have worshipped you accordingly."

This was due to their urge to come to grips with reality — an urge such as is found in every human being, the difference between one individual and another being only one of degree: in some, the urge is weak, in others it is strong.

Then, there are some deviations. Some people take certain material objects to be their goal in life and do their utmost to obtain them. But there is an internal evidence that they do so mistakenly. Before obtaining these material objects, they are highly enthusiastic about them. But as soon as they have them in their possession their enthusiasm turns to frustration for, with experience, they invariably find that what they have struggled for so hard, has failed to give them the desired sense of fulfillment. All these material things in this world are meant to fulfill only our physical needs. They have nothing to do with the purpose of our lives. This purpose can be only spiritual in nature, and not something material.

To achieve this purpose is the greatest quest in life. Everyone is motivated, consciously or unconsciously, by this demand of human nature, everyone at one time or another suffers from a sense of frustration, with or without sad experiences. To make one's life meaningful, therefore one has to discover its purpose. One should be extremely sincere and honest in this respect. Sincerity and honesty are an assurance of engaging oneself unremittingly in this pursuit, and never giving-up, until one has discovered the real purpose of human existence.

When a man succeeds in discovering this ideal, he becomes a person who is fit to be called a complete man, one who has succeeded in making his life purposeful, in the real sense of the word. Such a person has been called in the Qur'an: *Al-Nafs al-Mutmainna* (89:27). This means a soul at rest, in peace or in a state of complete satisfaction. That is, a man who wholeheartedly follows the divine way of life and is always fully satisfied, whether or not it is in consonance with his own desires. By showing such total willingness to surrender his will to the will of God, he attains that state of humanity which is at one with the creation plan of God. Such people will be rewarded with eternal paradise in the world Hereafter.

This will to search for the truth is implanted in everyone. But it depends upon every individual himself, whether or not he pursues this natural urge. Only through sincere pursuit will he discover the truth and thus make his life meaningful. For any kind of negligence or apathy in this regard, there is no excuse, whatever the circumstances.

Philosophy

Philosophy is the only discipline which, by its own definition, embodies the quest for knowledge and understanding of the nature and meaning of the universe as well as of human life.

But after a long search of more than 5000 years, to which the greatest minds of human history have been bent, it has failed to provide any definite answer to such questions.

Bertrand Russell was a great thinker of the present world, whose life spanned almost a century. He spent almost his entire life in reading and writing on philosophical subjects. But he failed to evolve any credible ideology. Because of this failure, one of his commentators remarks that "he was a philosopher of no philosophy." This is true not only of Bertrand Russell, but also of all other philosophers. Individually or jointly, they have failed to produce any philosophical system which might have provided a sound answer to the human dilemma.

The main concern of philosophy was to make a unified picture of the world, including human life. But the long history of philosophy shows that this still remains an unfulfilled dream. The Encyclopaedia Britannica in its 27-page article on philosophy and its history, admits that there seems to be no possibility of philosophical unification. The article concludes with this remark:

> In the contemporary philosophical universe, multiplicity and division still reign. (EB, Vol. 14:274 [1984])

Why this failure? This failure is not of a chance or intermittent nature, but seems to be a permanent feature of the philosophical approach to reality. The Qur'an has drawn our attention to this fact, saying:

> They put questions to you about the Spirit. Say: "The Spirit is at the command of my Lord and of knowledge you have been given only a little." (17:85)

This means that the problem stems from man's own shortcomings. The philosophical explanation of the world requires unbounded knowledge, whereas man has had only limited knowledge bestowed upon him. Due to these intellectual constraints man cannot uncover the secrets of the world on his own. So it is not the lack of research, but the blinkered state of the human mind, that stands as a permanent obstacle in the philosopher's path to reality. It is this human inadequecy which explains the unexplainable.

For example, suppose, in order to unveil reality and the law of life, the enquirer starts from a study of human settlements. After a detailed survey, he comes to the conclusion that since society is composed of human beings, he had better focus on the individual, and so he studies human psychology. But there he finds that, despite extensive research in this field it has resulted in nothing but intellectual chaos.

He ultimately finds that no unified system emerges from psychology. In despair of finding any solution to the problem, he turns to biology. His in-depth study of biology leads him to the conclusion that the whole human system is based on certain chemical actions and reactions, so, for a proper understanding of the human body he begins to study physics and chemistry. This study leads him to the discovery that, in the last analysis, man like other things, is composed of atoms. So, he takes to the study of nuclear science, only to arrive at the conclusion that the atom is composed of nothing but incomprehensible waves of electrons.

At this point man, as well as the universe, are seen as nothing but, in the words of a scientist, a mad dance of electrons. A philosopher ostensibly begins his study from a basis of knowledge, but ultimately comes to a point where there is nothing but the universal darkness of bewilderment. Thus a 5000-year journey of philosophy has brought the sorry conclusion that, due to its limitations, it is simply not in a position to unfold the secrets of the universe.

It is evident from the several thousand year-long history of philosophical inquiry, that philosophy has failed to give any satisfactory answer to questions concerning reality. Moreover, there is a growing body of evidence that philosophy is inherently incompetent for the task undertaken by it. The need, therefore, is to find some alternative discipline that may help us reach our desired intellectual goal.

Science

What is science? According to its definition "Science is a branch of knowledge concerned with the material world conducted on objective principles involving the systematised observation of, and experiment with physical phenomenon."

Science has divided the world of knowledge into two parts—knowledge of things and knowledge of truths. According to this division, science has confined its study only to a part of the world and not to the entire world. A scientist has rightly remarked that "science gives us but a partial knowledge of reality."

This means that science being confined in its scope to the physical aspect of the world, has kept itself aloof from higher spiritual matters. No scientist has ever claimed that science attempts to find out the absolute truth. All scientists humbly submit that the "search for truth" is not their target. They are simply trying to understand how the objective world functions and not why it functions. For instance, the chemistry of a flower may be chemically enalyzed, but not its odour.

Chemistry can describe how water may be turned into steam power, but not why a miraculous life-giving element such as water came to exist in our world. Similarly, while science is concerned with the biological aspect of man, it is not the aim of science to try to discover the secret of the strange phenomena commonly known as the mind and spirit.

Science has never claimed that its objective is to discover the total truth or absolute reality. The concerns of science are basically descriptive, and not teleological. Although science has failed to give a satisfactory answer to the quest for truth, it is not to be disparaged, for this has never been its motivation.

Many people had pinned their hopes on science providing them with the superior life they had sought for so long. But after more than two hundred years, it has dawned upon recent generations that science has fallen very far short of fulfilling man's hopes and aspirations, even in the material sense. Now it has been generally acknowledged that, although science has many plus points for human betterment, it has many minus points as well.

Science gave us machines, but along with them it also gave us a new kind of social problem: unemployment. Science gave us comfortable motor cars but at the same time it polluted the air, making it difficult for human beings to inhale fresh air, just as with the rise of modern industry, there came the pollution of life giving water. Production may have been speeded up, but at the cost of adversely affecting our whole social structure.

If the object of science was to provide man with the answer to his search for truth it had obviously failed. If the search for truth was not within the province of science, there was no reason for it to figure in such discussions at all. In other words, science cannot be legitimately blamed for not helping man to grasp the ultimate reality, for this was not something expected of it. Indeed the reality lies far beyond the boundaries of science.

Mysticism

What is mysticism? According to the Encyclopaedia Britannica, mysticism is a "quest for a hidden truth or wisdom." The Fontana Dictionary of Modern Thought, defines it thus: "Mysticism is the direct experience of the divine as real and near, blotting out all sense of time and producing intense joy."

Some people mistakenly think that mysticism is the answer to the search for truth. In fact, mysticism, to be more exact, is a sort of escapism. It seeks a refuge rather than the truth.

According to the mystics, the final state produced by mystical exercises is inner joy or spiritual bliss. The subject of the present volume is the search for truth. So far as this subject is concerned, mysticism is quite irrelevant to it.

1. The search for truth, by its very nature, is entirely an intellectual exercise. Its findings too are intellectual in nature. It is succesful when the seeker finds rational answers to the questions he poses about the universe and his own existence. The search for truth is not a vague matter. It begins from the conscious mind and also culminates there.

    The case of mysticism is quite different. Mysticism, essentially based on intuition, is not really a conscious intellectual process. As such, the mystical experience is more an act of spiritual intoxication than an effort to apprehend the truth in intellectual terms. A drug user undergoes an experience of inner pleasure which is too vaguely and unconsciously felt to be explained in comprehensible language. Similarly, what a mystic experiences is a type of unconscious ecstasy, which does not amount to a consciously sought after or properly assessable discovery. On the contrary, the search for truth is an intellectual exercise from beginning to end.

2. Mysticism, as popularly conceived, makes the basic assumption that the physical, material, and social needs of man act as obstacles to his spiritual progress. Therefore, mysticism teaches him to reduce his physical needs to the barest minimum; to renounce worldly and social relations; and if possible to retire to the mountains or jungles. In this way, he will supposedly be able to purify his soul. Thus, by giving up the world and by certain exercises in self-abnegation, a mystic expects to awaken his spirituality.

The educated community, however, does not find this concept of mysticism acceptable. A seeker aims at a rational explanation of the world and endeavours to discover a definite principle by which he may successfully plan his present life. Mysticism, on the contrary, teaches man to abandon the world itself; to depart from the world without uncovering its mystery. Obviously such a scheme amounts only to an aggravation of the problem rather than a solution to it.

3. The mystics can broadly be divided into two groups. Those who believe in God and those who do not. Non-believers in God assert that there is a hidden treasure in the centres of our souls. The task of the mystic is to discover this hidden treasure. But this is only a supposition. None of them has ever been able to define this hidden treasure or to explain it in understandable

terms. Tagore has thus expressed this claim made by the mystics:

> "Man has a feeling that he is truly represented in something which exceeds himself."

But this is only a subjective statement unsupported by logical proofs. That is why, in spite of its great popularity, no school of this mystical thought has so far produced any objective criterion by which one may rationally ascertain that the existence of such a hidden treasure within the human soul is a reality, and not an illusion. On the other hand, no well-defined law, or step-by-step practical programme, has been introduced by any individual or group that might help the common man reach his spiritual destination consciously and independently.

Moreover, mysticism makes the claim that the natural quest of man is its own fulfillment. It does not require any external effort to arrive at the perceived goal. In other words, it is like assuming that the feeling of thirst or hunger in man contains its own satisfaction. A thirsty or hungry person is not to trouble himself to search for water or food in the outer world.

4. Those (of this school of thought) who believe in God interpret this hidden treasure in terms of God. To them the inner contemplation of a mystic is directed towards God.

This concept too is rationally inexplicable, for, if such mystic exercises are a means to discover God, then, there should be genuine proof that God Himself has shown this way to find Him. But there is no evidence that this path has been prescribed by God. On the other hand, there is a clear indication that this course separates the seeker from God's creation and leads him to a life of isolation. This makes it plain that God cannot enjoin such a path to realization as would mean nullifying the very purpose of creation.

5. The mystics hold that although the mystical experience may be a great discovery for them, it is, however, a mysterious, and unexplainable realization which can be felt at the sensory level, but which cannot be fully articulated. According to a mystic: "It is knowledge of the most adequate kind, only it cannot be expressed in words." (EB/12:786)

This aspect of the mystical experience proves it to be a totally subjective discipline. And something as subjective as this can, in no degree, be a scientific answer to the human search for truth. Those who have attempted to describe the mystic experience have chosen different ways of doing so. One is the narrative method, that is, describing their point of view in terms only of claims, without any supporting arguments. Another method is to make use of metaphors. That is, attempt to describe something by means of supposed analogies. From the point of view of scientific reasoning, both the methods are inadaquate, being quite lacking in any credibility in rational terms, and are therefore invalid.

2

❦

Faith and Reason

It is through reason that man justifies his faith. Rational justification strengthens his convictions. Rational argument is thus an intellectual need of every believer. Without this he would not be able to stand firmly by his faith. It is reason which transforms blind faith into a matter of intellectual choice.

History shows that man has employed four kinds of argument to find rational grounds for his faith. Each of these reflects different stages in his intellectual development.

Natural Argument

The first kind of argument is one based on nature. That is, on simple facts or common experiences. This has been the most commonly used since ancient times. Some examples of this kind are found in the Qur'an, one of which relates to the Prophet Abraham. It is stated as follows in the Qur'an:

> Have you not considered him (Namrud) who disputed with Abraham about his Lord, because

God had given him the kingdom? When Abraham
said: 'My Lord is He who gives life and causes to
die,' he said: 'I too give life and cause death.'
Abraham said: 'So surely God causes the sun to rise
from the east, then you make it rise from the west.'
Thus he who disbelieved was confounded; and
God does not give guidance to unjust people.
(2:258)

We find another example of the argument based on
natural reasoning in the Qur'an:

Thus did We show Abraham the kingdom of the
heavens and the earth, so that he might become a
firm believer. When night overshadowed him, he
saw a star. He said: 'This is my Lord'. But when
it set, he said: 'I love not those that set.' Then when
he saw the moon rising, he said: 'This is my Lord.'
But when it set, he said: 'Unless my Lord guide
me, I shall surely be among those who go astray'.
Then when he saw the sun rising, he said: 'This is
my Lord. This is the greatest.' But when it set, he
said: 'O my people! Surely, I am done with what
you associate with God.' (6:75-78)

Argument of this kind may appear to be simple, but
they are invested with deeper meaning. For this reason,
they have been engaged in as much in the past as today.

Philosophical Argument

The second kind of argument is that first propounded
by Greek philosophers. Based on pure logic, it was so
popular in the medieval ages that Jews and Christians and
Muslims all incorporated it into their theological system.
Commonly known as First Cause, it may be summed up
as follows:

The world man observes with his senses must have been brought into being by God as the First Cause. Philosophers have argued that the observable order of causation is not self-explanatory. It can only be accounted for by the existence of a First Cause. This First Cause, however, must not be considered simply as the first in a series of successive causes, but rather as the First Cause in the sense of being the cause for the whole series of observable causes.

The Prime Mover or First Cause theory. Although obviously very sound, it has constantly been under attack from secular circles, and critics have raised a variety of objections. To begin with, they say that it is only guesswork, and not an undeniable fact. Some critics also object that the actions or free will of subatomic particles are uncaused; so, why not also the world as a whole? Moreover, even if all things in the world are caused, this may not be true of the world itself, because no one knows whether the whole is sufficiently like its parts to warrant such a generalization.

This is why some people think that the faith of Islam is not based on rational grounds. They say that Islamic belief can be proved only through inferential argument and not through direct argument. They assert that in Islam there is only secondary rationalism and not primary rationalism. But modern science has demolished this notion, as will be shown in the last part of this chapter.

Spiritual Argument

Yet another argument is that which is based on spiritual experience. Some people, who engage in spiritual exercises and have spiritual experiences, say that when they reach the deeper levels of the human consciousness, they find an unlimited world which cannot be described in limited language. They insist that this limitless, unexplainable phenomenon is nothing but God Almighty Himself.

The critics say that even if this spiritual state is as real as is claimed by those who enter it, it is still a subjective experience; that it conveys nothing to those who have not experienced the same spiritual state.

All the above arguments are in one way or another inferential in nature and not of the direct kind. In view of this fact, the critics hold that all faiths, including Islam, have no scientific basis. They contend that Islamic theology is not based on primary rationalism, but on secondary rationalism.

However, these contentions appeared to be valid only by the end of the nineteenth century. The twentieth century has closed the chapter on all such debates. Now, according to modern developments in science, one can safely say that religious tenets can be proved on the same logical plane as the concepts of science. Now there is no difference between the two in terms of scientific reasoning. Let us then see what modern scientific reasoning is all about.

Scientific Argument

Religion, or faith, relates to issues such as the existence of God, something intangible and unobservable, unlike non-religious things like the sun, which has a tangible and observable existence. Therefore, it came to be held that only non-religious matters might be established by direct argument, while it is only direct or inferential argument which can be used to prove religious propositions.

It was believed, therefore, that rational argument was possible only in non-religious matters, and so far as religious matters were concerned, rational argument was not applicable at all. That is to say, that it was only in non-religious areas that primary rationalism was possible, while in religion only secondary rationalism was applicable.

In the past, arguments based on Aristotelan logic used to be applied to faith. By its very nature it was an indirect argument. Modern critics, therefore, ignored such arguments as unworthy of consideration. That is why religion was not thought worthy of being paid any attention by rational people. This state of affairs presented a challenge not only to other religions but to Islam as well.

About five hundred years ago, with the emergence of science, this state of affairs did not change. All the scientists in the wake of the Renaissance believed that matter, in fact, the entire material world was something solid which could be observed. Newton had even formed a theory that light consisted of tiny corpuscles. As such, it was possible to apply direct argument as an explanation of material things. Similarly, even after the emergence of modern science, this state of affairs prevailed. It continued to be believed that the kind of argument which is applied to apparently tangible things could not be applied in the case of religion.

But by the early twentieth century, specifically after the first World War, this mental climate changed completely. The ancient Greek philosophers believed that matter, in the last analysis, was composed of atoms. And the atom, though very tiny, was a piece of solid matter. But with the breaking of the atom in the twentieth century, all the popular scientific concepts underwent a sea change. The theories about faith and reason seemed relevant only while science was confined to the macrocosmic level. Later, when science advanced to the microcosmic level, it underwent a revolution, and along with it, the method of argument also changed.

So far, science had been based on the proposition that all the things it believed in, like the atom, could be directly explained. But when the atom, the smallest part of an element, was smashed, it was revealed that it was not a material entity, but just another name for unobservable waves of electrons.

This discovery demonstrated how a scientist could see only the effect of a thing and not the thing itself. For instance, the atom, after being split, produces energy which can be converted into electricity. This runs along a wire in the form of a current, yet this event is not observable even by a scientist. But when such an event produces an effect, for instance, it lights up a bulb or sets a motor in motion this effect comes under a scientist's observation. Similarly, the waves from an x-ray machine, are not observable by a scientist, but when they produce the image of a human body on a plate, then it becomes observable.

Now the question arose as to what stand a scientist must take? Should he believe only in a tangible effect or the intangible thing as well, which produced that effect. Since the scientist was bound to believe in the tangible effect, he had no choice but to believe in its intangible cause.

Here the scientist felt that direct argument could be

applied to the tangible effect, but that it was not at all possible to apply direct argument to the intangible cause. The most important of all the changes brought about by this new development in the world of science was that it was admitted in scientific circles that inferential argument was as valid as direct argument. That is, if a cause consistently gives rise to an effect, the existence of the intangible cause will be accepted as a proven fact, just as the existence of the tangible effect is accepted because it is observable. In modern times all the concepts of science held to be established have been proven by this very logic.

After reaching this stage of rational argument the difference between religious argument and scientific argument ceases to exist. The problem faced earlier was that religious realities, such as the existence of God, could be proved only by inference or indirect argument. For instance, the existence of God, as a designer (cause) was presumed to exist because His design (effect) could be seen to exist. But now the same method of indirect argument has been generally held to be valid in the world of science.

There are numerous meaningful things in the universe which are brought to the knowledge of human beings, for which no explanation is possible. It has simply to be accepted that there is a meaningful Cause, that is God. The truth is that, without belief in God, the universe remains as unexplainable as the entire mechanism of light and motion is without belief in electric waves.

Thus, the option one has to take is not between the universe without God and the universe with God. Rather, the option actually is between the universe with God, or no universe at all. Since we cannot, for obvious reasons, opt for the latter proposition, we are, in fact, left with no other option except the former, that is, the universe with God.

In view of the recent advancement in scientific reasoning, a true faith has proved to be as rational as any other scientific theory. Reason and faith are now standing on the same ground. In fact, no one can legitimately reject faith as something irrational, unless one is ready to reject the rationality of scientific theories as well. For, all the modern scientific theories are accepted as proven on the basis of the same rational criterion by which a matter of faith would be equally proved true. After the river of knowledge has reached this advanced stage, there has remained no logical difference between the two.

3

❀❀

The Concept of God

In 1965 in Lucknow I met a university Professor, a Doctor
of Philosophy, who had turned atheist. The subject of our
conversation was the existence of God, during which he
asked: "What criterion do you have to prove the existence
of God." I replied that I had a valid criterion and that it was
exactly the same as is employed in science to prove any
natural fact. Bertrand Russell has aptly said there are two
kinds of knowledge: knowledge of things and knowledge
of truths. So far as the "things" are concerned it is possible
to apply direct argument to them. But inferential arguments
alone can be applied to prove "truths," as relating to the
laws of nature. Inferential arguments are held to be valid
in science, that is, to admit the existence of some "reality"
on the basis of the existence of things. On the basis of this
reality, Bertrand Russell has acknowledged that the
"argument from design" brought forward by religious
people is a valid argument, according to science. The
argument from design sets out to prove the existence of a
designer from the existence of design.

By the first half of the twentieth century people used to debate over the existence of God. But by the end of the twentieth century this is no longer considered a debatable topic. Now in academic circles the existence of God is held to be a fact. Particularly after the Big Bang theory, this matter has been almost settled.

Now we are right, scientifically, in saying that the choice for us is not between the universe with God and the universe without God. Rather the real choice is between the universe with God or no universe at all. Since, from the scientific viewpoint, we are not in a position to opt for no universe at all, we are compelled to choose the universe with God.

As regards the scientific evidence on the existence of God, perhaps the first notable account was that prepared by Sir James Jeans, titled *The Mysterious Universe*, published in 1930. Many important books have subsequently come out on this topic, which describe how all the fields of the science of the universe point to the existence of God. Here I would like to refer to a very valuable book on this subject, consisting of forty articles written by qualified western scientists. It is titled *The Evidence of God in an Expanding Universe*, and is edited by John Clover Monsma.*

The truth is that both revealed and scientific knowledge equally prove that there is a God of this universe. And that God is only one. Not believing in God is as illogical as believing in many gods. In this present world man is given freedom for the purpose of being tested. Everyone is free

---

* First Indian edition (1968) printed by M.E. Eapen, at GLS Press, Bombay-75, Distributed in India by Pocket Books Distributing Co. II, Oak Lane, Fort, Bombay-1.

to say what he wants to and to believe in anything of his own free will. But so far as reason is concerned the only rational concept is that of one God. Everything else is irrational. No valid argument exists in its favour.

Once a group of young men in an Indian town were discussing whether God existed or not. Even after a long debate the matter could not be settled. Finally, they agreed to refer the matter to a certain pious Muslim scholar of the same town, who came there at their invitation. He stood among the youth and simply recited this verse from the Qur'an:

> "Is there any doubt about God, the Creator of the
> heavens and the earth?" (14:10)

The result was miraculous. The youths were left speechless. They found this argument from the Qur'an so convincing that they needed no further arguments to believe in God. How did it happen that assertion alone was sufficient to bring them to belief? It is because God is self-subsisting. He needs no proofs for His existence. The reason for God being self-evident is twofold. Firstly, the existence of the universe itself is a proof of the existence of God. Secondly, man's existence in itself is a proof of God's existence. Therefore, man believes in God, because he is bound to believe in Him. His inner nature speaks for God. Hence, most often, a simple assertion about the existence of God suffices for a man with an unbiased mentality to believe in God. One cannot afford to deny God, as that would be tantamount to a denial of one's own nature. At the same time, in the external world man sees clear evidence of God in nature all around him, day in and day out. God is so evident that any denial of God becomes artificial. That is why those who apparently reject God, also come to believe in God, when confronted with their own utter helplessness. (31:32;10:22)

The concept of God handed down to man by the Prophet is one of pure monotheism, that is "There is no god but one God." This Prophetic concept has been briefly set forth in a short chapter of the Qur'an:

> Say: He is God, the One God. The Eternal,
> Absolute. He does not beget nor was He begotten.
> And there is none equal to Him (Chapter 112)

However, in every age all sorts of concepts have been prevalent. These may be divided into two categories.

> One God versus many gods
> A Personal God versus an impersonal God

There are again several kinds of beliefs about God. Some believe in two gods, one of good and the other of evil. Some believe in three, as in the form of the trinity, a construct of the Christians. There are others who believe in multitudes of gods, as in Hinduism.

Now, of these concepts which should be held right and which wrong? The Qur'an gives us a clear assertion on this subject: There are only two forms of credible knowledge, that is, revealed knowledge and scientific knowledge. (46:4)

Let us first take revealed knowledge. When we make a survey of revealed scriptures, the first question that arises is which one of them is to be regarded as authentic? Apparently, in the world of today, there are many religious books which are said by their adherents to enshrine God's revelations. But when these books are judged on the basis of history, we find that none of them can sustain their credibility on purely historical grounds. We have no way of knowing, as a matter of historical record, precisely when and how these books came into existence, what their original language was, how they were preserved after the First Giver, how they reached later generations of followers — all these questions remain unanswered. These books are thus believed by their adherents to be holy scriptures, without their having any historical proof of this.

In this non-historical museum of "revealed" scriptures, the Qur'an is the only divine book which comes up to the standard of history in every respect. The Qur'an has every kind of historical credibility and authenticity, so that one may believe in it with full confidence.

This means that if an individual wants to find out the concept of God according to revealed knowledge, he can trust only the Qur'an to be the authentic source. It is a fact that, the Qur'an is the only existing divine scripture which provides a reliable source of learning the true concept of God.

When we refer to the Qur'an on this subject, we find that, according to revealed knowledge, there is only one true concept of God, and that is pure monotheism. That is, God is only one. He has no partner, no equal. He is eternal and beyond time and space. He alone is the Creator and Sustainer of all things. (2:255)

So far as the concept of three gods, or the trinity, is concerned, it is highly illogical in every respect. It is not proved by any revealed source. Even today it is merely a creed of the Christian Church. In neither the Old Testament, or the New Testament, held sacred by Christians, is there any clear mention of the concept of the trinity. In their own sacred scriptures the trinity is an alien creed.

So far as reason then is concerned, the concept of the trinity is not rationally understandable. In terms of the trinity, God is at the same time three in one and one in three. This is an inconceivable mathematical riddle, which none of the greatest of mathematicians can solve. That is why when a Christian professor of an Indian university was once asked by a student to explain the trinity, he had this to say:

> If you ask me I do not know, if you do not ask me
> I know.

The truth is that the concept of the trinity is wholly unproved so far religious scriptures are concerned. It is likewise entirely baseless judging by the criteria of knowledge and reason. Keeping this reality in view, it will not be wrong to say that this concept is so unfounded that, *prima facie*, it stands rejected.

Now let us talk of scientific knowledge. Scientific knowledge provides an academic verification of this concept of the one God. It affirms that God cannot be more than one, the concept of many gods not being understandable to a scientist.

The world discovered by science is a wholly unified world. All the parts of the present world are so interlinked with each other that it is impossible to separate them from one another. In such a world the concept of more than one God is quite alien. For instance, if the sun, the air, water, human beings and the earth had not been governed by one and the same Creator, a world of the present kind would never have come into existence. For instance, if the sunshine reached the earth unhampered, without there being the atmosphere to neutralize its harmful rays, the sun would be a killer instead of a source of life. If the gases in water were not in their present proportions, no living organisms could ever have come into being on the earth. If the size of the earth were half or double the present size, in either case civilization on earth would have been well nigh impossible.

There are countless things in the world. But everything exists in such proportions as will give the maximum benefit to life on earth. None of the things on this earth are out of proportion. This shows that there is only one God— the Creator and Sustainer of this world. If there were different gods for different things, then, this perfect balance could never have been possible. In ancient times people believed that there were numerous forces controlling the universe. Newton reduced these forces to the following four:

gravitational force, electromagnetic force, strong nuclear force, weak nuclear force.

However, the extraordinary unity that scientists found in the world was incompatible with the notion that it was being controlled by four forces.

That is why the scientists have been trying to reduce the four forces to one. Their efforts were crowned with success in the second half of the twentieth century. It is now generally believed that there cannot be four forces controlling nature, but only one. This has led to the formulation of the Single String Theory by scientists.

This goes to prove that the concept called *tawheed* (oneness of God) in revealed knowledge is fully borne out by scientific knowledge as well—that there is only one God, not many gods controlling this world.

4

✻⟨ᕙᕗ⟩✻

Religion

Let us now come to religion. Scholars have generally believed that in the search for truth, the most reliable source is religion. That is why in every age the majority of human beings have been associated with one religion or the other. And today, this is still the case.

Why is it that people take religion to be a reliable source of truth? The reason is that the teachings of religion are based on a special source such as no other discipline enjoys. This special source is that of divine revelation. God created the universe. He knows best its creation plan. He has full knowledge of which path in this world leads to success and which path leads to failure. Therefore, God-given guidance is entirely trustworthy.

After the creation of the universe, when man first inhabited the earth, God decreed that in every age and in every nation, there would be certain individuals who would be raised as prophets to guide mankind to the path of God. God, Who has absolute knowledge, sent His guidance to man. He did this by means of revelations which he bade the angels convey to the prophets in the form of divine books. These are the sacred books on which the religions of the world are based.

These religious books have guided man in all ages. In every era a large number of people have found in them light for their minds and solace for their hearts. The goal of religions has always been to give man a proper knowledge of His Creator, so that he may properly understand the universe and the purpose of human life in it.

Religion informs man of his beginning and his ultimate end. It enables man to lead his life in this world according to the creation plan of God, so that he may be entitled to the divine rewards.

About two dozen Prophets have been mentioned in the Qur'an by name. In a *hadith*, the number of these Prophets and messengers has been put at 1,24,000. However, with the exception of the Prophet Muhammad ﷺ, no authentic historical record is available of any other prophet. But, in principle, we have to believe that God's prophets came to every nation and in every age, whether or not we have any record of them.

A religious system generally includes beliefs, worship, ethics, social behaviour, etc. One of the important contributions of a religious system is that, it provides man with a life-long centre around which his intellectual and emotional being may revolve.

Religion offers man an ideology in which he may believe with all his heart and all his soul. It gives man the conviction that he is in communion with Almighty God. On finding a religion, man feels that he has become a co-traveller with the rest of the universe. He has become a member of the universal brotherhood.

Religion gives man a practicable system of life. He finds a course which he may properly pursue day and night. Having found a religion, man feels as if he now understands the purpose of his life; he undergoes the same experience—but with greater intensity—as a traveller does on reaching his destination.

Religion, the science of life, is an eternal source of inspiration and guidance to man. As such it acts as a spur to spiritual and intellectual growth. Its absence from human life, would eliminate all possibility of man's following a course that would lead him towards a total and meaningful development of his personality.

Religions Other than Islam

The Qur'an and the Bible both tell us that, ever since the advent of man on earth, God has sent His Prophets to convey His message to mankind. According to a *hadith*, from Adam to Jesus Christ, more than one hundred thousand prophets have come to the world. Every prophet brought God's religion and communicated it to his people. This divine scheme has continued in every age and in all places.

All these religions brought by God's messengers were one and the same. Originally there was no basic difference between one religion and the other. But it happened that none of the concerned peoples were able to preserve the teachings of their prophets. Either these religions survived in a distorted form, or they vanished without leaving any trace. Moreover, contemporary historians failed to attach any importance to these prophets or their teachings. For this reason few of these prophets found their place in the annals of history. The only exception is that of the final prophet, Muhammad, peace be upon him.

This blackout of history was so complete that even the prophets of later periods of history received scant mention in contemporary records. For instance, Jesus Christ came to the world two thousand years ago, and so little is known about his life that a western scholar was once constrained to remark: "Historically, it is quite doubtful whether Christ ever existed at all."

Due to the paucity of reliable documentation, all the previous religious scriptures, except that of Islam, have lost their historical credibility. By rational standards all other religions have assumed the status of a set of dogmas rather than that of a chronicled event. One can believe in them only as a matter of faith and not as a fact of history. However, the position of Islam in this regard is totally different. Muhammad, the Messenger of Islam, as acknowledged by all well-known historians of the world, was born in the full light of history, and whatever he said or did in his life-time has been recorded in considerable detail.

The Qur'an, the last word of God, has been preserved just as it was first revealed to the Messenger of Islam. The textual originality and purity of the Qur'an is incomparable and unquestionable. Islam, as a whole, passes the strictest criteria of higher criticism and historical verification. So, when one opts for Islam, one does so as a matter of history, not simply as a matter of faith.

One can safely say, therefore, that for a seeker after the

truth, there is no whole range of options. He has only one choice to make. And that is the choice of Islam: the only religion having true historical credibility.

For instance, according to our belief, Abraham and Moses were Prophets of God. Abraham was born in Iraq and Moses in Egypt. Yet the annals of the respective countries are devoid of any mention of these great prophets. We find no reference in the ancient history of Iraq to Abraham. Similarly, Egyptian history makes no mention of Moses.

In a similar way, as testified to by the Qur'an, Jesus was a prophet. Even Gautam Buddh is considered a prophet by his followers. But neither Jesus Christ nor Gautam Buddh come up to the strict standards of history. For example, there are long periods of Jesus's life about which nothing is known, and the stories of the New Testament were not written until more than a century after his death. Three languages— Syriac, Greek and Hebrew— were prevalent during the time of Christ, yet we have no way of knowing, with certainty, about the language in which he communicated his message to his people.

In the times of Gautam Buddh, Pali and Sanskrit were in vogue. But there is no historical evidence as to which language he spoke. The actual words spoken by Gautam Buddh are not on record. There are some who claim to have proofs that Gautam Buddh spoke in Pali, but it has not been established by the scholars of Buddhism.

The reason is that, in ancient times, before the age of the press, the concept of historiography was very limited. At that period it was only a record of kings and generals; only events relating to victory and defeat were considered worth recording. All other incidents remained unrepresented and since the prophets or the reformers were not associated with events of a political nature, the historians did not consider their lives worthy of being immortalized.

The case of the Prophet Muhammad ﷺ was exceptional in that is was quite different from that of the other prophets. Circumstances were such that he became involved in all kinds of political events, and he and his companions were able to usher in a revolution bringing about sweeping changes in the political and the social order of the time. Naturally the events of his life came to be recorded in the contemporary history and thus he became an essential part of history. In this way, by historical standards, the Prophet Muhammad ﷺ became a historical personality, in the full sense of the word.

Because of non-existent documentation, all the other religions and their founders have come to be considered lacking in credence. One who examines these religions objectively feels that he is studying beliefs rather than history, for the personalities associated with these religions, their religious scriptures and their teachings have been demonstrated to be scientifically and historically unreliable.

An Encyclopaedia of the Hindu religion, published under the title *Encyclopaedia of Hinduism*, drew the comment from a scholar that it would be more aptly titled *Encyclopaedia of Hindu Mythology*. This is the case with all religions. All the faiths save Islam may be classified as mythologies rather than religions in the scientific and historical sense.

The subject matter of ancient alchemy and modern chemistry is one and the same. Yet we all know that there is a basic difference between the two. Alchemy was based on unproved speculations, while modern chemistry is based on facts proved by strictly scientific methods. This same difference is found between Islam and other religions, the latter being like ancient alchemy, whereas the former is like modern chemistry.

This difference is so evident that no one can fail to notice it. One who sincerely makes a comparative study of religions of both kinds will inevitably discover it. Hence Islam is the only choice for those who seek a religion with a credible historical base.

5

※ᴥᴥᴥ

Islam in Brief

What is Islam? This is a vast subject. In this chapter we shall give a brief account of some of its basic aspects in the light of the Qur'an and *hadith*.

True Guidance

The Qur'an leads us to the true guidance. In this connection, we quote a passage from the Qur'an:

> Allah is He besides Whom there is no god, the Ever-living, the Self-subsisting by Whom all subsist; slumber does not overtake Him nor sleep; whatever is in the heavens and whatever is on the earth is His; who can intercede with Him but by His permission? He knows what is before men and what is behind them, and they cannot comprehend anything out of His knowledge except what He wills. His knowledge encompasses the heavens and the earth, and the preservation of them both does not tire Him, and He is the Most High, the Great. There is no compulsion in religion; truly the right way has become clearly distinct from error;

therefore, whoever disbelieves in Satan and believes in God, shall indeed lay hold of the firmest handle, which shall not break off. God is All-Hearing and all-Knowing.

God is the guardian of those who believe. He leads them from darkness to the light. As for those who disbelieve, their guardians are false gods who lead them from light to darkness; they are the inmates of the fire and in it they shall abide forever. (2:255-257)

Now, let us try to visualize the above quoted Qur'anic passage, in its applied form, so that we may have an idea of what kind of individual, what kind of society and what kind of State would respectively emerge, if Islam were consciously accepted and practised in letter and spirit.

A. Individual

Islam is the religion of the universe. The Qur'an says:

Are they seeking a religion other than God's when every soul in heaven and on earth have, willingly or by compulsion, bowed to His will? (3:83)

This means that submission to God is the only true religion for both man and the universe. All the things on the earth or in space are following God's commands to the letter. The revolution of the stars, the flowing of water, the growing of trees, in short, all things following the same course which was determined for them by God. Nothing is allowed to deviate from the divine path. The Qur'an says:

The sun is not allowed to overtake the moon, nor does the night outpace the day. Each swims along in its own orbit. (36:40)

The same is required of all human beings. Everyone should strictly obey the commands of God without any deviation or alteration. The Prophet Muhammad ﷺ has declared:

> A believer with his faith is like a horse with its tether. The movement of the horse is restricted to the length of its tether. So is the case with the believer. His words and deeds are all restricted by the limitations set by his faith. (*Mishkat al-Masabih*, vol. 2/1226)

The true Muslim leads a highly disciplined life, always adhering to the set of do's and don't ordained by God Almighty. He is entirely pure in speech, and even subordinates his intention and thinking to the will of God. He always feels himself to be a servant of his Lord. The Qur'an depicts the true Muslim thus:

> And the servants of the Beneficent God are they who walk on the earth in humbleness, and when the ignorant address them, they say: "Peace." And they who pass the night standing and prostrating themselves before their Lord. And they who say: O our Lord! ward off from us the punishment of hell, for surely its punishment is everlasting. Surely it is an evil abode and (evil) place to stay. And they who, when they spend, are neither extravagant nor parsimonious, but keep the golden mean. And they who do not call upon any other god besides Allah and do not kill, which Allah has forbidden, except in the requirements of justice, and (who) do not commit fornication and he who does this shall meet with evil; his punishment shall be doubled on the Day of Resurrection, and he shall abide in abasement forever; unless he repents

and believes and does good deeds; for them Allah will change his evil deeds to good ones; and Allah is Forgiving, Merciful. And whoever repents and does good shall surely return to Allah. And they who do not bear witness to what is false, and when they hear what is profane they maintain their dignity. And they who, when reminded of the signs of their Lord, do not fall down thereat deaf and blind. And they who say: 'O our Lord! grant us in our wives and our offspring the joy of our eyes, and make us examples to those who fear you.' These shall be rewarded with lofty places in paradise because they were patient, and shall be met therein with greetings and salutations. There they shall abide forever: a blessed dwelling and blessed resting place. Say (to the unbelievers): Little cares my Lord for you if you do not invoke Him. But Now that you have indeed rejected (the truth), His punishment is bound to overtake you. (25:63-77)

B. Society

The foundation of society in Islam is based on mutual well wishing. In chapter *Al-Asr* (The Time) the Qur'an says:

By the time, verily Man is in loss, except for those who believe and do good works and exhort one another to truth and to patience (103:1-3)

How should a Muslim live in a society? The answer is given in one of the *hadith*: "If any one of you sees an evil in society, he must rectify it by his own hand. And if he has no capacity to do so, he should do it by his tongue. And if he is unable even to discourage it, then, let him condemn the same in his own heart." (*Bukhari*)

A society based on these principles will naturally be a place in which good will flourish as a result of mutual reminding, and the roots of evil, if not totally eradicated, will dry up due to public discouragement. As the truth is openly propagated and the virtue of patience is highly recommended in this society, there will definitely prevail a peaceful atmosphere which is prerequisite for the healthy growth and development of both the individual personality and the social system at large. It is only in an atmosphere of such peaceful social order that the rights of individuals and communal harmony are ensured, and the higher values of brotherhood, cooperation and altruism are sincerely observed; and, finally, the projects of common welfare, progress and prosperity are successfully achieved.

To sum up, when the ideals of Islam are consciously put into practice by its adherents, there will emerge a society that will be appreciably more secure, free of violence and naturally cooperative, progressive, prosperous, good enhancing and evil-resisting.

C. State

What is a state? It is an organised political community under one government. Islam does not prescribe any particular form or structure of the State. Nevertheless, Islamic teachings seem to be so comprehensive that they embrace all essential issues of life including the State and its related national or international problems as well.

What is an Islamic State? A State governed by Muslims is not necessarily an Islamic state. Apart from its monotheistic doctrinal basis, an Islamic State would, in practice, be identified with the sumum bonum principle of 'no-compulsion.' No compulsion should be exercised, either before or after the gaining of power. For power gained through compulsion or power used for compulsion in any sphere whatsoever, particularly in religious matters, is strictly prohibited and condemned in Islam. That is why the coercive forms of States, though governed by Muslim dictators, have never been considered ideal Islamic States by the scholars of Islam. Islam, moreover, does not allow its followers to rebel against any established State, even though it may not seem to be in accordance with the Islamic Ideal. Compulsion on the part of the State should never be resisted by means of counter-compulsion, i.e. it has to be countered through negotiation, backed up by conviction. This ensures such stability of law and order as will subsequently help promote Islamic values, and this may gradually prepare a firm ground for a real Islamic State to stand on.

To establish an ideal Islamic State is not the main target of Islam, as is wrongly projected by some groups of Muslims. An Islamic State is something that may ultimately emerge from a society consisting of sincere, practising Muslims, and its government may take any workable form, —this being neither predictable nor pre-determinable. Such a State, according to the Qur'an (24:55), is a worldly reward of Allah granted to His righteous servants, when He wills, and not a direct target towards which the Muslim community must struggle.

To conclude, Islam begins when one discovers God as the ultimate truth. This results in a spiritual transformation which leads to new thinking and new sentiments —indeed to the emergence of a whole new personality. A new man is born: he is quite different from what he was before. He now becomes a combination of spirituality, compassion and tranquillity. This is like an intellectual and spiritual revolution. This inner transformation finds expression in his external behaviour, in worship, in character, in social relations, etc. To produce a person like this is the main target of Islam. All other aspects of Islam hinge on the fact that man lives in a society, and the greater the number of such individuals in a society, the greater the changes brought about at the social level. This process leads to what may be called the social system of Islam.

This revolution among individuals and society goes on developing until, conditions being favourable, it culminates in what is termed the Islamic State. This process is mentioned in the Qur'an:

> God has promised to those of you who believe and
> do good works that He shall make them masters
> in the land as He made their ancestors before them,
> and that He shall certainly strengthen the religion
> which He has approved for them, and that He shall
> certainly change their fears to a feeling of security
> and peace. Provided they worship Me. (24:55)

In a garden it is the individual tree which has the real existence. The garden is only a collective manifestation of a number of trees. This is true also of man. In the Islamic scheme, it is the individual—who is a real part of the body of Islam while society and the State are only its relative part.

Those individuals who have undergone spiritual transformation are called "rabbani" in the Qur'an. Where there are "rabbani" individuals in considerable numbers, the "orchard," that is, Islamic society, and the state, will come into existence on their own.

6

The Creation Plan of God

The Famous historian, Edward Gibbon, observed: "Human History is little more than a register of the crimes, follies and misfortunes of mankind." Other historians have also arrived at similar conclusions, for the ideal existence envisioned by philosophers is nowhere reflected in human societies. Orientalists who have made an in-depth study of human history have remarked that, as regards the human failure to achieve the ideal society, Islamic history is no great exception.

Orientalists hold that, although the history of the first phase of Islam—known as the golden age—no doubt presents a better picture than that of other periods, it too fails to measure up to the ideal. During the life of the Prophet, owing to the antagonistic activities of the hypocrites internally and the Jews and idolaters externally, Madinah, the city of the Prophet, could never in any significant sense be converted into an area of peace. After the Prophet's demise, and shortly after the first caliph, Abu Bakr, had been appointed to be the leader of the Muslims, most of the Arab tribes revolted. It was only when force was used that they were prevailed upon to re-enter the Islamic fold.

Subsequently, in almost every period, unfavourable developments repeatedly proved to be hindrances to the formation of the ideal society. During the times of Umar, the second caliph, a secret lobby in Madinah, working towards the extirpation of Islam, finally succeeded in having the caliph assassinated. Afterwards the age of open opposition set in. The third caliph, likewise, was publicly murdered. The reign of Ali, the fourth caliph, was marked by civil war in which thousands of precious lives were lost and the caliph himself was martyred.

Given the state of affairs, thinkers and philosophers have always expressed pessimistic views about human history, holding it to be an ongoing tragedy: events have shown that, in this world, the building of the ideal human society is well-nigh impossible.

The reason for this pessimistic view of history does not lie in history itself, but in our flawed approach to the subject. Our criterion to study history is not the correct one, for it has been formulated by human beings. The only valid criterion, in the light of which we should study human history, is that laid down by our Creator. The right way to understand this matter is, therefore, to discover the creation plan of the creator and then attempt to study history within its framework.

From a study of the Qur'an, we learn that for a proper understanding of human society the central idea is not ideal society, but it is human freedom. Man has been granted full freedom of speech and action in this life the reason being that he has been placed in this world by the

Almighty for the purpose of being tested. As a prerequisite for this test, man is at liberty to deny God, to kill prophets and to oppose the *da'is* (messengers) of truth. Given such a state of affairs , human freedom would have to be withdrawn altogether in order to bring an ideal society into existence. And God, in accordance with His plan of creation, would never under any circumstances abrogate human freedom. The particular nature of human existence on earth has been thus explained in the Qur'an:

> We offered Our trust to the heavens, to the earth and to the mountains, but they refused to accept the burden. Man undertook to bear it, but he has proved foolish and unjust. God will surely punish the hypocrites, men and women, and the unbelievers, both men and women; but God pardons believing men and believing women. God is Forgiving and Merciful. (33:72-73)

'Trust' in the above verses refers to the freedom of choice with which man has been entrusted. The earth and the heavens have neither such freedom nor any will-power of their own. They are compelled to adhere to the laws of nature laid down by God for all eternity. But man has no such compulsion. He is totally free in word and deed.

From other verses in the Qur'an, we learn that, according to the Creation plan of God, what is of actual importance in this world is the building not of an ideal society but of ideal individuals. (67:2) The ideal human society will, therefore, come into existence not in this world, but in the world Hereafter — referred to in the Qur'an as *Darus Salam* (the Home of Peace). The actual obstacle to the building of the ideal society in this world is the presence everywhere of rebellious and insolent people. In the heavenly society of the Hereafter, all such evil-doers will be separated from good people; the heavenly society will then be comprised only of virtuous souls. Only in heaven then will it be possible to create an ideal society.

The error in the thinking of secular philosophers derives from their desire to construct in this present world the ideal society — the society which, according to god's scheme of things, is going to become a reality only in the world of the Hereafter. The most formidable obstacle to the emergence of an ideal society is human freedom, but thanks to the exigencies of God's trial of humanity, human freedom is not going to be taken away. The ideal society will thus remain a distant dream.

According to the Qur'an, the truth has been fully set forth in this world. Now it is up to man to put his faith in it or to deny it (18:29). At another point the Qur'an says:

> It rests with God to show the right path. Some turn
> aside from it, but had He pleased, He would have
> given right guidance to you all. (16:9)

The Qur'an further observes; Had your Lord pleased, He would have made mankind a single nation. But only those to whom He has shown mercy will cease to differ. To this end He has created them. The world of your Lord shall be fulfilled: 'I will fill Hell with jinn and men all together.' (11:118,119)

This freedom granted to man by his Creator is the reason why a society with uniformity in all its aspects could never be produced in human history. If in a society there are virtuous people, there are wicked people as well. The unworthy have never ceased to create disturbance, even the societies founded by the prophets are no exception.

That is why despite the existence of good individuals in this world, a good society could never become a possibility.

However, this is not a matter of evil, or even of deficiency. The truth is that the recurrence of disturbance and dissension in society is essential to the realization of the Creation Plan itself, for good people of the highest calibre are produced in unfavourable rather than in favourable situations.

We learn from the Qur'an that man was born to an existence fraught with toil and strife. (90:4) The Qur'an, addressing the human race, has this to say: 'Go hence, and may your descendants be enemies to each other.' (7:24) In this world, man has no choice but to lead a life which is marred by trial and tribulation, opposition and enmity till the coming of Doomsday.

This human condition has not come about by accident. This is exactly in accordance with the divine scheme of things. God has created this world in order to select those individuals who are capable of inhabiting heaven. These worthy inhabitants of paradise are invariably produced under abnormal rather than normal circumstances. Human beings should therefore will continue to face unfavourable circumstances in order that desirable people will go on being produced for such a selection.

The Qur'an states: Do men think that once they say: 'We are believers,' they will be left alone and not be tried? We tested those who have gone before them. God knows those who are truthful and those who are lying (29:1-3). In a similar vein the Qur'an says: Did you suppose that you would go to Paradise untouched by the suffering which was endured by those before you? Affliction and adversity befell them; and so battered were they that each apostle, and those who shared his faith, cried out: 'When will the help of God come?' His help is ever near. (2:214)

There is another verse to this effect: Did you suppose that you would enter Paradise before God has known the men who fought hard and the steadfast? (3:142). Yet again the Qur'an addresses Muslims in these words: Did you imagine that you would be abandoned before God has had time to know those of you who have fought valiantly and served none but Him and His Apostle and the faithful? God is cognizant of all your actions (9.14)

The truth is that in this world what is desirable to God is not the Ideal Society but the Ideal man. And as we learn from the Qur'an, such an individual is produced in conditions of 'severe affliction,' (Qur'an, 33:11) and not in normal, peaceful circumstances.

God looks with favour upon those human beings who, finding themselves in the midst of a jungle of theories and ideologies, are able to discern the truth and then to persevere in their adherence to it. He gives His approval to those human beings whose faith remains unshaken even in the face of severe problems and dire adversity; whose hearts, even when they are subjected to all manner of persecution, are untainted by negative sentiments; who when threatened with calamity, do not lose heart, but undergo such a process of brainstorming as will lead to their intellectual development; who even when faced with such untoward events as are likely to divert them from the Straight Path, remain staunch in their faith in God; who feel the great tumult of the awakening of spirituality in their hearts, bringing them closer to God.

The man most desirable to God is one worthy of inhabiting the refined and ideal world of Paradise. Such a person, the rarest of rare phenomena, is greater than all that is great in the Universe. Such a human being takes a new birth. He is born, not in peaceful circumstances but in great strife and turmoil. He faces darkness in this world, so that he may live in the eternal light of the Hereafter. He treads a thorny path in this life, so that he may enjoy a flower-filled environment in the afterlife. Here he suffers loss, so that he may be blessed with the joys of recovery in the Hereafter. He patiently bears the deprivation of the pleasures and comforts of this world, so that he may be entitled to a place in the eternal Paradise of heavenly bliss.

Such a precious soul cannot come into being in a vacuum. Nor can he develop in the normal atmosphere of society—no matter how closely approaching the ideal that society may be. It is only in the jungle of adversity that such a soul can emerge; there is no other possible breeding ground.

What philosophers describe as social evil is a training ground devised by the Creator to produce human beings of great moral and spiritual character. That is why, in every period of human history, mankind has been faced with all manner of conflict and dissension. The true believers, the virtuous and, in particular, the prophets, have invariably found themselves in unpropitious situations. There is a *hadith* to this effect: "When God loves a people, He puts them to the test."

Unfavourable circumstances are not peculiar to non-Muslim societies; in one way or another, they have always been a part of Muslim societies too. In ancient times, the prophets were born among idolaters and deniers and were subjected to severe persecution by their contemporaries. We learn from the Qur'an that the Prophet Moses was likewise threatened with mental torture and physical agony, even although he had been sent to the People of the Book, that is, to the Jews. (33:69)

The Prophet Muhammad ﷺ established a properly organized state in Arabia, later known as the *Khilafat-e-Rashida*, and ruled successively by the four rightly guided caliphs. But even during this ideal period of Islam, the state continued to suffer from a variety of severe problems. Indeed, there is no period of the Islamic State which can be pinpointed as one in which Muslims led their lives in a state of perfect peace and normalcy.

This is not due to any deficiency in the Islamic State, but rather to the exigencies of the "training course" established by God Himself for the moral discipline of human beings. As mentioned above, it is not part of God's plan that an ideal society should be formed in this world in which people will lead peaceful lives. According to God's scheme of things, what is of actual importance is the preparation and formation of individuals. This unavoidably takes place in an atmosphere, not of peace and tranquility, but of turbulence and turmoil.

In the present world, neither at the national or communal level, do we possess the moral and physical resource which are essential to the construction of a high standard society. However, we do have the means to build the ideal character in individuals, and this is an ongoing reality— as a requirement of God's Creation plan, which is concerned not with the building of a heavenly society, but the building of the heavenly individual who is fit to dewll in the ideal society of paradise.

Looked at in terms of the ideal society, the history of Islam would appear to have its darker, negative side. But if seen in terms of the development of individuals, this same history would appear to have a very positive, bright side. The ideal society or the ideal state may not have come into being but, throughout Islamic history, there has never been any dearth of individuals of great moral and spiritual calibre. Indeed, the annals of history may have little to show in terms of ideal societies, but their pages have been made resplendent with the thoughts, words and deeds of ideal individuals.

7

❦

Discovery of Islam

Once a Muslim scholar from the UK visited India to give a lecture on: 'Islam and the West.' During the question hour, an Indian Muslim asked: 'You have given us so much information about Islam and the West, now, would you please tell us what the Muslims should do, when in the minority, in countries such as India?' The scholar remained silent for a while and then replied: "It is, indeed, a difficult question. In Islam we find a model for a position of strength. But, there is no model in Islam for the position of modesty." This is not just a stray remark. In fact, it illustrates the way of thinking prevalent almost all over the Muslim world today. It clearly shows the mindset of today's Muslims. Consciously or unconsciously, they look to their glorious history in order to understand their status and role in the world. Their mentality is such that when they find a prominent model of strength, they naturally conclude that what Islam stands for is world-wide Muslim political dominance. It is this attitude which prevents them from penetrating the veil of their glorious history to seek guidance directly from the Qur'an and Sunnah. Had they done so, they would certainly, have succeeded in finding role models for all human positions including that of modesty. They would further have realized that it is not the political but the ideological spread of Islam through peaceful *da'wah* work that the Muslim Ummah has to struggle for everywhere and under all circumstances.

Contrary to the prevalent misconception that Islam failed to provide its followers with any model of a low-key position, an unbiased study of the Prophet's biography will reveal that up till the conquest of Makkah in the 8th A.H., 20 of the 23 years of his life as a Prophet, were spent in exactly what is nowadays termed a state of mdoesty. When, chronologically, more than three quarters of the Prophetic mission portrays a picture of humility, what is it that makes one remark that there is no Islamic model for Muslim minorities in India or elsewhere? The fact is that such people are so overwhelmed by the political glory built up during the later period of Muslim history, that their eyes are totally blinded to the glory of the modesty in the life of the Prophet.

This shift in later history of drawing inspiration from political glory instead of from the Qur'an and Sunnah, has, unfortunately, blurred the general vision of present-day Muslims to such an extent, that the original Islam has turned for them into an alien religion. They proudly claim that Islam is a complete code of life and that their Prophet had set a perfect role model for all times to come, yet due to their own misdirected approach, they are unable to find any model for the position of modesty which is comparatively much more important than the model for a position of strength, as it is popularly called.

This state of affairs is entirely in accordance with the prophetic prediction: "Islam began as a stranger. And, finally, it will again become a stranger. Let, then, the strangers be blessed." (Muslim) It would be no exaggeration to say that the original version of Islam has literally become totally unfamiliar to both Muslims and non-Muslims alike. Islam, has thus, to be rediscovered. And to rediscover Islam, we have first of all to discover what the factors are that have made Islam a stranger in the world today. In the following pages, the reader will find a thorough analysis of the historical and political reasons for the tragic phenomenon of the alienation of Islam as predicted in the *Hadith*.

Why Islam alone

We seldom hear the adherents of other religions complaining about their faiths being misunderstood. For instance Hindus, Buddhists and Christians do not hold that their respective religions are badly understood. One reason is that they do not mix their religions with communal politics, and do not generally try to advance their own worldly interests in the name of their religions — as present-day Muslims are doing on a large scale.

One who studies Islam, directly from its sacred scriptures, is astonished to find that the original Islam is totally different from what it is now generally held to be. Other religions are known to people as they are, hence the need to rediscover them does not arise. The problem of misapprehension applies therefore exclusively to Islam.

There is a great need to study Islam from its original scriptures in order to re-discover it in its original form. In modern times many books have been published with the aim of removing misunderstandings about Islam. One title is as follows:

'Islam, the Most Misunderstood Religion'.

But titles such as these are not in accordance with the actual state of affairs. These books start with the premise that non-Muslims have mistakenly come to regard Islam as a religion of intolerance and violence and then they attempt to remove these misapprehensions. But the actual question to be addressed is why there should ever have been such misunderstanding. It has to be conceded that it is based not on some allegation but rather on the fact that the Muslims of today, in almost every country, repeatedly display violence and intolerance towards others. They have adopted this course of action in the name of Islamic movements or Islamic *Jihad*. Were Muslims to do so in the name of their own communal interest and people attributed that to Islam, this would amount to misunderstanding based on an allegation. But when Muslims themselves attributed their activities to Islam, it becomes a case of *proper understanding and not that of misunderstanding*.

Furthermore, the educated class of modern times is obsessed with the concept of anthropology, which treats religion as a social phenomenon instead of as a vehicle for revealed truth. Therefore, according to their way of thinking, they naturally come to regard the activities of Muslims to be Islam itself. And their thinking is further confirmed when they find that Muslims engage themselves in these activities in the very name of Islam.

Given this state of affairs, the real task to be performed is to differentiate between Islam as such and Muslims. It should be made clear that Islam and Muslims are not necessarily one and the same thing, so that one must differentiate between Islam and Muslims. Islam is an ideology. One who adopts this ideology in full is a Muslim, otherwise he is not a Muslim. It is essential that Muslims be judged in the light of Islamic ideals: Islam should not be judged in the light of what Muslims do in the name of Islam.

Prophetic Perspective

In a *hadith* the Prophet Muhammad ﷺ observed: My generation is the best one, then the second generation and then the third generation. (*Sahih Muslim*, 8/550)

This means that Islamic virtue was at its peak in the first generation, and that there was a decline in righteousness through the second and the third generations. This stage is known in the history of Islam as the period of the Prophet's companions and the period of Prophet's companions' companions.

There is nothing mysterious about it. Degeneration, a law of nature which applies to every group, set in after the first generation itself. By the third generation, the roots of Islam had weakened and by the fourth generation the characteristics of the first generation had been considerably diluted. This process went on until after a few centuries that period commenced when, we do find individuals in considerable number who had imbibed the true spirit of Islam, but society on the whole was found drastically lacking in the features of the early Islam.

This is what is meant by Islam becoming "a stranger," as in the above-quoted prediction of the Prophet. In latter times this difference has become so marked that the Islam of the early days has come to appear strange to the Muslims of today. Some basic reasons for this transformation are outlined below:

Separation of Spirit and Form

The first reason for this difference lies in the separation of the spirit from the form. In later generations the form remains intact but the spirit is lost, rather like a fruit with its skin intact but altogether devoid of pulp.

For instance, in the first phase *iman* (faith) meant realization of God, while in later times *iman* becomes synonymous with the recitation of the creed of Islam (*kalimah*). In the early phase *ibadah* (worship) meant *khushu,* (spiritual devotion) but in later times it becomes synonymous with a set of rituals. In earlier times *Akhlaq* (good moral character) meant unconditional good character, but in later times it becomes synonymous with the kind of character, whose goodness or badness depends upon the good or bad conduct of others.

If, in the early period of Islam, a position of trust was identified with responsibility, in the later period it becomes associated with honour and prestige. In the early phase, the ideology of Islam was highlighted, while in the later phase the history of Islam replaced the ideology. In the first phase, Islam was an issue of duty; in the second phase, it became an issue of pride. In the first phase, the Quran was a book of *tadabbur,* (deep contemplation), whereas in the second phase, it became simply a book for recitation. In the first phase, following in the footsteps of the Prophet was given the utmost importance but in later times, the Prophet was glorified as a national hero, so that Muslims might assert their own superiority over other nations. While the thinking of the first generation was that they could earn paradise only on the basis of their personal deeds, the people of the later period came to hold that mere association with the Ummah (community) was enough to secure them paradise. People of the first generation turned to the original texts as preserved in the Qur'an and Sunnah to seek guidance in every matter; while people of the later generation refered to the commentaries and interpretations produced afterwards. In the first phase self-reckoning and criticism were appreciated, but in later times criticism became a taboo as Muslims became reluctant to accept their own faults, considering themselves above any shortcoming.

Due to these differences, the religion of the first phase of Islam became an unknown religion for the people of the later phase. Indeed, when they were called to the religion of the first phase, they found it so unfamiliar to their thinking and practices that they became dire opponents of such a call. However, there is no doubt that one who loses his popularity among the people as a result of calling them to the original Islam will have a great reward reserved for him by God in the Hereafter.

Communalization of the Religion

Another reason for public alienation from the real Islam is that the faithfuls fall from the high pedestal of principled religion to the level of communal religion. Then, this communal agenda is Islamized, the ideals of

Islam being replaced by communal aspirations. This is the result, in modern times, of Muslims being faced with many kinds of communal problems, such as the usurpation of their land, deprivation of political power, cultural invasion, exploitation in terms of economic resources, etc. And there are many other similar communal problems from which present day Muslims are suffering at the hands of their opponents.

All over the world, Muslims have launched movements on these scores. In some places they take the form of protest and demands, while in others they develop into armed conflicts. If such activities have any justification, it is purely communal. Muslims fight for their communal objectives, but they call it Islamic jihad. Their leaders form political parties, they enter into violent conflict with other rulers in order to gain power, but they carry out all these activities in the name of Islam. Power play, pure and simple, is given the name of Islamic politics. The so-called Islamic jihad is the most glaring example of engaging in non-Islamic activities under the banner of Islam. In different parts of the world, wherever Muslims are engaged in fighting for their own communal purposes they inevitably call their activities Islamic jihad. The harm done by such violent jihad has multiplied 1000 fold due to the modern media's selective coverage of news. Since hot news is more profitable than soft news, examples of Muslim *jihad* are seized upon by the media as grist to the mill. This has distorted the image of Islam to such an extent that, today, Islam and violence have become synonymous.

A state of affairs has developed in which Muslims have come to believe that the cause of Islam can be served only through jihad activism, that is, armed struggle. With this mindset, they are unable to understand the significance of peaceful struggle. Anyone who talks in terms of peace and tolerance finds his integrity in question. Any attempt at making them understand the importance of peaceful struggle is seen as a conspiracy to keep them from performing jihad as a "religious duty." It is thus an extremely difficult task to call Muslims to peaceful Islam. Such a mission involves the risk of being discredited among one's own co-religionists. In consequence, the call, goes unheeded.

The Veil of Interpretation

One reason for original Islam becoming alien is that as time went by self-styled interpretations of the Qur'an and Sunnat gradually placed a veil over the original content of these texts. A time came when the original Islam was completely obscured from view. The wrong, man-made interpretations took the place of revealed guidance. In later times, people mistakenly took them to be the real Islam.

In the early phase of Islam people derived their religion directly from the Qur'an and Sunnah, therefore, their association with the original Islam remained intact. But the interpretations and explanations of later days served only to obscure the original teachings. The natural beauty of Islam disappeared. The Qur'an and Sunnah now turned into relics instead of being instruments of guidance. Thus the religion came to be based on latter-day interpretations and explanations instead of on the original scriptures.

How did this corruption set in in the literature produced by the later generations? The answer is that certain people, having a command over the language, were able to acquire a superficial knowledge of the scriptures but were unable to understand them in depth; for this realization (ma'arifa) is required. When one finds religion at the level of realization, one is endowed by God with the wisdom (hikmat) to be able to understand the deeper meaning of the words of the scriptures. On the other hand those who are not blessed with this special gift of wisdom, have nothing by which to understand Islam, except their own preconceptions.

They begin to interpret religion according to their own mindset. The result is that, although they refer to the Qur'an and sunnah, their interpretations have little bearing on the original texts. Religious degeneration ensues in which they appear to follow Islam but actually stray far from its spirit. They fail to differentiate between God-sent religion and man-made interpretation. At this point, one who calls people to the original Islam becomes an alien among his own people. He fails to gain popularity even among those already in the Muslim fold. However, losing popularity in this world for the sake of God will earn him a greater reward in the life Hereafter. For, when the image of Islam had been distorted, it was he, who was ready to take all the risks involved in the process of reviving its original form.

One great loss created by these additions to the original Islam was the shift in emphasis. Some important teachings of Islam were relegated to the background— for instance, concern for the larger humanity, *da'wah*, patience, etc. *Da'wah* is the greatest mission of the Muslim Ummah, for, although prophethood came to an end with Muhammad (PBUH) the mission of the Prophet has not yet come to an end. The mission continues through the *Ummah*, as a matter of religious duty. It would be no exaggeration to say that without the performance of this duty, its very credibility of being the Muslim Ummah would become doubtful. Strangely, indeed, *da'wah* found no place in the literature of the centuries after the Prophet. Neither has it been mentioned anywhere in the Muslim agenda of today. The classical commentaries of the Qur'an *(Tafsir)* also fail to give any prominence to *da'wah* as a concept. In books of *hadith* too, we find chapters on all subjects except *da'wah*. The same is true of *fiqh* (Islamic jurisprudence) in whose texts we do not find a chapter on *da'wah*.

According to the Qur'an, the exercise of patience (*sabr*) is a deed which makes man eligible for the highest reward (8:46); the patient man will be rewarded "beyond measure" (39:10) But the interpretation that gained popularity in later times was that the injunction of *sabr*, patience, had been abrogated and replaced by *jihad* (in the sense of qital, fighting). Thus, one who studies these books, gathers the impression, that consciously or unconsciously, patience might have been important in the past, but that nowadays it has lost its relevance. Now *jihad* (in the sense of *qital*) and not *sabr* is of the foremost importance.

It follows that whenever a reformer calls Muslims back to their duties concerning *da'wah* and *sabr*, they become antagonistic to such a call, because they have become conditioned to finding it alien to their thinking.

The Obsession with Historical Glory

As mentioned above, one of the major reasons for the original Islam becoming an alien religion among the

Muslims is that for latter day generations the basis for the Islamic ethos became the later history of Islam instead of the Qur'an and Sunnah. Muslims found their glorious history far more attractive than the Qur'an and Sunnat. For them they were just sets of words. Their history, on the contrary, gave them an immense sense of pride, as it was full of imperial grandeur and conquests. Although they continued to pay lip service to the Qur'an by reciting it, they were, in fact, lost in the glories of Islamic history. Gradually they came to associate themselves and Islam with this grand history: instead of the Qur'an and Sunnah, history became their chief source of inspiration.

This change of the source of inspiration wrought immense harm. When the Qur'an and Sunnah are one's intellectual sources it is modesty that is bred in the mind, whereas if one takes history as one's intellectual source, pride is bound to be generated.

If the Qur'an and Sunnah are taken to be the true sources of knowledge of God's will, all mankind, in the words of a *hadith*, will be regarded by the believers as God's family; the whole of humanity will become their concern: whereas, when the mind is shaped by history, Muslims see themselves as rulers, and others as subjects. If they derive Islam from the Qur'an and Sunnah, then all God's creation— even a blade of grass—will appear to them as God's signs. Whereas when history is the source of their Islam, the forts and palaces of their kings become signs of grandeur and glory to them. This is exactly what has happened with the latter day Muslims. Almost all the activities of Muslims in present times bear testimony to this fact. The speeches of their leaders, the books of their writers, the poetry of their poets, seem to centre on their glorious history. Their writers and speakers provide them food for thought about historical glory rather than divine glory. This is the reason why in modern times a large number of books have been written by the Muslims bent on the celebration of history, while perhaps not a single book has been produced on the majesty of God Almighty.

Given this state of affairs, when a reformer arises to call Muslims to the religion of the Qur'an and Sunnah, his voice naturally appears strange to his hearers. For they feel that this person is calling them to a position of modesty, whereas their religion (that is, history) aims at placing them in a position of strength. In such an atmosphere, the words of the reformer will impinge as worthless, alien and unacceptable.

8

❧❦❧

The Man Islam Builds

The man Islam aims to build is one in whom a two-fold activity is set in motion at the same time, one form of activity being internal and the other external. The result of this twin activity, is that the spiritual side of his nature develops in parallel with his intellectual advancement, both processes going on unhampered. On the one hand there is a strengthening of the moral fibre by which his personality assumes its permanent shape, and on the other, there is a broadening of his intellectual horizons.

Internal Development

How does the Islamic way of life set off inner activities in man? In this, the mainspring is the concept of accountability. Islam brings man to the realization that God Almighty is omnipresent and omniscient so that he has the feeling that for all his words and deeds—even intentions, he is accountable before Him. And after death he will have to face the divine court of justice, where the whole record of his life will be examined. And then, according to its verdict, he will be sent either to eternal hell or eternal Heaven. This feeling surging within him is so powerful that it shakes the entire human personality. A *hadith* thus admonishes the individual: Reckon yourself before being reckoned with. Weigh yourself before being weighed. And prepare yourself for the Great Appearance on Doomsday. (*Al-Tirmidhi*)

The consciousness of the presence of God activates all of the brain cells of the individual. A hunter once remarked: If you are walking through a jungle, and all of a sudden you notice a live tiger standing, in a nearby glade your blood stream will turn into a blood storm.

This is what happens when we stand in the presence of a tiger. At every moment Islam brings man to the realization not only of the Creator of the lion, but also of the Creator of the entire universe. One can judge when the thought of the presence of a tiger turns man's blood stream into a blood storm, how great a storm the thought of the presence of the Creator of the lion, that is, God Almighty, will be produced within a believer.

Therefore, by his own inner compulsion, the believer becomes a man of character and a staunch believer. For him it becomes impossible to be immoral or unjust or dishonest in his conduct to his fellow men.

This concept of the presence of God is no negative matter. This is a wholly positive reality. This is because God is not simply a source of power. He is also a source of mercy. The storm brought about by the awareness of the presence of God awakens not only the feeling of fear, but a strong feeling of hope as well. Similarly, the feeling of the presence of God becomes a perpetual incentive for the positive development of the human personality. This, in Islamic terms, is called a spiritual revolution. In short, belief in Islam makes accountability to God man's greatest permanent concern. The potential of spirituality latent within man is activated by his belief to the ultimate extent; this turns him into a spiritual superman. But the feeling of the presence of God Almighty also cuts man down to size. 'And man cut to size' is the ultimate phrase in the spiritual dictionary. Such a man succeeds to the utmost degree in finding all those things that he ought to experience at the spiritual level. He becomes a man of God through and through.

External Activities

The Islamic man is one who, in consonance with his spiritual development, experiences constant intellectual activity which results in the most intense brain storming. The intellectual awakening, or intellectual development of an Islamic man is so extensive that he becomes cerebrally activated to the highest possible extent. What is that external factor which stimulates this kind of intellectual activity in the Islamic man? It is *da'wah* work.

According to the Qur'an, Prophet of Islam is the final Prophet. Although no Prophet is going to come after him, the mission of the Prophet must continue. The Ummah of the Prophet, charged with carrying on this mission for posterity, is thus addressed in the Qur'an: And thus We made you an intermediary nation so that you might bear witness against the people and the Prophet might testify against you. (2:143)

A commentator of the Qur'an has interpreted this as follows: Muslims are intermediary between the Prophet and the nations of the world. (*Al-Tabari*) In conformance with this, *da'wah* work is obligatory for the Muslim Ummah. It is their essential duty to receive the divine message of the Prophet and convey it to the rest of humanity. It is not simply an act of annunciation. It is the most important struggle. Because of this the Qur'an says: Do with them the great *jihad* by the help of the Qur'an (25:52)

The Qur'an is a book, not a weapon. "Great *jihad* with the Qur'an" means a great religious endeavour; *da'wah* work is thus a great ideological struggle. It is a supreme intellectual effort which stretches to the utmost the mental capacity of the human being.

Intellectual Development

Da'wah is a strictly non-political mission. But it is an extremely difficult task to perform, because it invites challenges from virtually all sections of society. The *da'i* says: "Here is the truth with a capital T, and success in this world as well as in the world hereafter depends on the acceptance of this truth, so man has no choice but to accept it." This kind of claim is highly provocative, eliciting reactions from every ideological group—religious, materialist, secular, atheist, etc.

The man with a mission throws down a challenge which provokes a response. A challenge-response-mechanism becomes operative which stimulates continuous interaction, involving questions and answers, discussions and dialogues. It is during this interaction that the process of intellectual development begins.

As a mission, *da'wah* work by its very nature is divine. Because of this people with a mission are bound by their code of ethics to respond in a positive manner to their audiences regardless of the latter's misconduct. At all costs, they must, as a matter of principle, avoid all friction. As the Qur'an says: "Certainly, we (the Prophets) would bear with patience your persecution of us." (14:12)

This positive behaviour on the part of people engaged in the *da'wah* mission prevents them from succumbing to hatred for and violence against the other party. That again ensures that their intellectual growth and development will go on uninterruptedly. No situation whatsoever will halt this process of peaceful *da'wah* and, subsequently, the inner progress of those involved in it will continue ceaselessly.

The Prophet Muhammad ﷺ once said: "Beware of the wisdom of *mu'min* (a believer), because he sees with the light of God." How is it that a *mu'min* becomes a man of wisdom, in such a superior sense? It is because his faith makes him pious and God-fearing. In his state of piety, he undergoes the inner experience which psychologists call brainstorming. This helps activate his potential to the full extent. The result is miraculous: if, before, he was a man, now after this brainstorming, he becomes a superman.

Then comes *da'wah*, that is, the call to Islam. According to the Qur'an, *da'wah* is the great *jihad*. Why is *da'wah* the great *jihad*, or great struggle? Because it is a universal mission. It is a most serious task. It engages one's entire capacities throughout one's whole life. Every time one is faced with intellectual challenges, one is bound to give a strong response.

Thus, *da'wah* becomes an extensive course of action through which one's personality develops day by day, until one reaches the highest level of intellectual and spiritual development.

Iman (faith) and *da'wah* are two basic levels of Islam. If iman is a superior ideology, *da'wah* is a superior course of action. Iman purifies one's mind and soul, while *da'wah* imbues one's personality with a sublime probity. One who adopts Islam as a universal mission, in both the ideological and practica¹ sense, is morally activated to the maximum possible extent and this course, slowly but surely, leads him to reach the highest pinnacle of humanity.

Stating the relationship between man and true religion the Qur'an says:

> So you set your face towards the true faith uprightly, the upright nature with which God has endowed man, and let there be no alteration in God's Creation. That is the right religion, although most men may not know it. (30:30)

This means that every human being is created by God to be capable—as a matter of his natural constitution—of accepting the religion of truth. The Unity God is a truth, arrived at intuitively, and is plain to every man of common sense, unless he perverts himself by the different prejudices which he receives from his environment. Islam is thus the natural religion that a child left to itself would develop. A western writer, Lady Cobbold, has rightly described it:

Islam is the religion of common sense.

When this potential is realized, it results in the emergence of a new man. What kind of character is possessed by this new man is made clear by the following *hadith:*

Nine things the Lord has commanded me:

Fear of God in private and in public;
Justness, whether in anger or in calmness;
Moderation in both poverty and affluence;
Joining hands with those who break away from me;
and giving to those who deprive me;
and forgiving those who wrong me;
and making of my silence meditation;
and my words remembrance of God;
and taking a lesson from my observation.

(Razin)

This *hadith* gives a complete picture of the man Islam wants to build.

9

The Islamic Way of Life

The Islamic way of life, in a word, is a God-oriented life. The greatest concern of a Muslim is God Almighty. The focus of his whole life is *Akhirah*, that is, the ideal world of God. He always obeys divine injunctions in every aspect of life. His life becomes a practical expression of the Qur'anic verse:

> Take on God's own dye. And who has a better dye than God's? And we are His worshippers. (2:138)

'Taking on God's dye,' means being of a 'godly character' in all the personal, social and economic affairs of one's life. The following pages of the chapter are devoted to portraying various aspects of this 'godly' character as personified in a Muslim individual whose words and deeds in family matters, or with respect to earning one's livelihood and whose dealings with other members of society, always seem to be distinguishably 'dyed in the divine hue.'

Iman (Faith)

By accepting *iman* one enters the fold of Islam. But Iman is not simply a recitation of *kalima* (creed of Islam). According to the Qur'an, it is *ma'arifah* (5:83) that is, realization. Thus realization of truth is the door to Islam. When one discovers that Islam is truly God's religion and that it is the same truth one has been seeking all along, one undergoes a unique experience of realization which is known in Islamic terminology as *ma'arifah.'*

Making any kind of discovery revolutionizes a person's life but when this discovery is of the truth with a capital T, this intellectual revolution becomes synonymous with the emergence of a new life in the individual.

This kind of intellectual revolution is no simple event: it turns a man into a superman, and gives him the greatest mission of his life. It regulates his life in such a way that no part of it remains unaffected. He begins to see all of humanity as his family and the entire universe as his abode. Such a discoverer becomes a maker of history rather than a product of history.

This is the stuff of *iman*. And it was this *iman* which enabled the Prophet and his companions to produce, as one historian remarked, "the most miraculous of all miracles."

Ibadah (worship)

Ibadah, or worship, is not simply the observation of a set of rituals. It is more a profound kind of religious experience. In fact, it is the physical and spiritual expression of the human personality on a higher plane of consciousness.

Addressing man, the Qur'an says, "Prostrate yourself in adoration and bring yourself closer (to God)." (96:19) The Prophet Muhammad ﷺ was once asked 'What is the essence of *ibadah*? He replied: "The worship of God as though you are seeing Him. Or if you are not seeing Him, He is seeing you."

There are two kinds of ibadah, or worship, in Islam, the first kind of *ibadah* have been prescribed at specified times—*salat, sawm, zakat, hajj,* (prayer, fasting, almsgiving, pilgrimage) These forms of devotion are called the pillars of Islam. Then there are unspecified forms of *ibadah*, which consists of *dhikr* and *fikr* (3:191), meaning to remember God with feelings of fear and love.

This second form of *ibadah* aims at mental activation of the human soul so that he may be enabled to see God's signs in everything he comes across in his daily life. This is the *ibadah* or worship, which is obligatory for every Muslim throughout his life.

Akhlaq (morality)

What is morality? It is to live among one's fellow men according to the moral teachings of Islam. The essence of Islamic morality is thus set forth given in a *hadith*: "Behave with others as you would like them to behave towards you." (al-Bukhari) By nature everyone knows of what sort of conduct he approves and of what sort he disapproves. So to follow this generally accepted moral criterion in relation to others is essentially Islamic morality.

Islam differentiates between social manners and social character. Social manners are based on the principle 'Do as they do.' But Islamic morality is based on the formula of unilateral and unconditional positive conduct. 'Do good to others, even if they are not doing good to you.' (al-Tabarani)

The Qur'an portrays Muslims as individuals who "repel evil with good." (28:54)

Similarly, the Prophet Muhammadﷺ advised a Muslim to "do good to those who harm you." (al-Tirmirdhi) The Prophet Muhammadﷺ was the true embodiment of the finest moral character. Addressing the Prophet, the Qur'an declares: "Surely you have a sublime character." (68:4)

So great an importance has been attached in Islam to moral character that it has been set up as a criterion by which to judge all other Islamic virtues. If one is good in relation to other human beings, that will serve as evidence that one also is good in relation to God.

The Prophet Muhammadﷺ puts it thus:

> "One who is not grateful to man cannot be grateful to God either." (Al-Bayhaqi)

Social Relations

A. Individual Responsibility

To preserve society from instability and keep it in a perpetually reformed state, Islam has given a basic commandment, which has been mentioned at many places in the Qur'an. One such Qur'anic verse runs: "(Believers are those) who enjoin what is good and forbid what is evil." (9:112) The same point has also been repeatedly made in a number of traditions such as the following: "A believer ought to open the gate of good and close the door of evil." (Musnad Ahmad).

This commandment has been misrepresented by certain self-styled advocates of Islamic revolution as being political in nature. But this is not so. It is entirely non-political. It only indicates that every member of society should have a strong sense of his responsibility towards society. No one should remain indifferent on seeing the perpetration of evil or injustice. He should feel the pain of others in his own heart. He should rise in support of the rights of the oppressed. When one sees someone engaged in the calumny and slander of others, he should attempt to stop him from doing so. He should make the iniquity known to other people, so that the culprit may be compelled by means of public pressure to desist from indulging in such evil acts.

Every member of society should consider the upholding of virtue to be an essential duty. The greatest concern of every individual should be to see that goodness flourishes in society and that evils are uprooted from it. Before any evil takes roots , it should be nipped in the bud.

This task of enjoining good and forbidding evil has to be performed with the utmost gentleness and well wishing rather than with harshness and violence.

That is why this social responsibility has been linked with acts of worship in Islam. For instance, with reference to prayer, the Qur'an says: "Surely, prayer keeps (one) away from indecency and evil." (29:45)

B. Family Life

A sane society, from the Islamic point of view, is but an extension of a sane family. Even human society at large is nothing other than a single family gradually extended throughout history. That is why Islam has greatly emphasized the significance of family life being disciplined and well organised so that it may play its part in maintaining social stability.

A family begins when a male and a female decide as members of society to live together under one roof. However, Islam does not allow such a relation between a man and a woman, unless it is based on a legitimate marital contract which is basically meant to be a guarantee of a life-long partnership of rights and duties, and not merely a temporary entertainment. Hence, there is no room in Islam for what is known, as pre-marital or extra-marital affairs between the two sexes. And this is one of the reasons that we do not find in Islamic society broken homes, illegitimate children, neglected or abandoned parents, etc.—phenomena that are prevalent in secular societies.

Through the institution of marriage Islam aims at building a society free from anarchy, instability, indecency, violence and crime, especially in relation to youngsters. Marriage, when conducted and maintained on the lines laid down in the Qur'an and Sunnah, provides an organised unit in the form of a 'home.' In that way, the succeeding generations are brought up and nurtured physically, morally and mentally in a healthy atmosphere and under the supervision of loving and concerned parents. This training at home helps the children enter society equipped with a deep sense of responsibility, respect for human values and other qualities, such as sincerity, which are essential for the better construction and development of any social system. A society composed of such homes or training units, will never suffer from the chaos and destructive instabilities from which modern societies are suffering nowadays.

Guidelines for a healthy, happy and meaningful marital life, along with the rights and duties of parents and other members of the family, occupy a considerable space in both the Qur'an and *Hadith*. A few references in this regard are given below:

1. "Men should approach women with the sincere intention of entering into wedlock with them, not committing fornication" (4:24)

2. "And your Lord had commanded you to serve none but Him, and to show goodness to your parents. If either or both of them reach old age with you, show them no sign of impatience and do not rebuke them, but speak to them a generous word. Treat them gently and with compassion, and say: "O my Lord! have mercy on them as they brought me up when I was little.'" (17:23-24).

3. "No parents have ever given to their children any gift better than a good moral education." (*Al-Adab al-Mufrad*).

4. "My Lord has enjoined me to do nine things," the Prophet once said, and one of them, he stressed was "keeping on good terms even with those relatives who cut off ties of kinship." (al-Hakim).

C. Legitimate Livelihood

So many social evils can be directly attributed to either some members of society having an insufficient means of livelihood or others having an excess of wealth. Islam urges that one earns one's livelihood by all possible but lawful means, so that one's essential needs are properly met on the one hand, and one does not remain dependent on others, on the other. According to the Qur'an and *Hadith*, the greed for more and more, niggardliness, holding money back to centralize it in one or a few hands, are the main roots of all criminal and destructive tendencies in human society. That is why virtues such as contentment, moderation, simplicity, altruism, spending on charity and sharing one's happiness with others are so highly and repeatedly recommended in Islam.

Conversely vices like extravagance, selfishness, monopolistic practices, exploitation, usury and all unfair means of money-making are strongly condemned and prohibited. How to deal with the problems of earning a livelihood in accordance with the Islamic way of life? The answer to this question may be summed up in the following points:

(a) Avoidance of transgression. God Almighty has declared in the Qur'an: "Eat of the good things we have given for your sustenance, and do not transgress with respect to them." (20:81)

(b) Self-reliance. One should try one's utmost to earn one's daily bread by one's own efforts, without being dependent on anybody else. The Prophet Muhammad ﷺ is reported to have said repeatedly: "The best food one has ever had is that which one has earned with one's own hands." (Abu Dawud)

(c) Avoidance of niggardliness and spending in charity. When one is fortunate enough to earn even more than it takes to meet one's own needs, one should not try to be parsimonious with one's earnings. Instead, one should rather extend a supporting hand to less fortunate or even destitute members of society. Otherwise, one's wealth will become a curse for oneself rather than a blessing. Hence, the Prophet Muhammad, peace be upon him, used to say in his regular prayers: "O Allah, give a good compensation to one who spends in charity and cause destruction to one who holds his wealth back." (Nasai)

(d) Contentment. To attain inner peace and real happiness, one has to remain content with what one has been able to earn independently and lawfully. The Prophet Muhammadﷺ says in this respect: "Indeed, he has attained eternal success and prosperity who accepted Islam, and God has filled his heart with contentment towards whatever he was given." He also said: "A little that suffices is much better than a surfeit that causes disturbance." (Al-Bayhaqi)

(e) Simplicity. Last, but not least, an important Islamic principle concerning one's livelihood is simplicity. The Prophet's own life style was a unique example of simplicity. In one of his sayings he has even considered it one of the signs of true faith (Ibn Majah). In another *hadith*, he warns his companions: "Stay away from the luxurious life. For the servants of God do not indulge in luxury." (*Musnad Ahmad*)

10

✻❀✻

Islam As it is

Islam is a religion of peace in the fullest sense of the word. The Qur'an calls its way 'the paths of peace' (5:16). It describes reconciliation as the best policy (4:128) and states that God abhors any disturbance of the peace (2:205)

The root word of Islam is *'silm'*, which means peace. So the spirit of Islam is the spirit of peace. The first verse of the Qur'an breathes the spirit of peace. It reads:

> In the name of God, the Most Merciful, the Most compassionate.

This verse is repeated in the Qur'an no less than 114 times. It shows the great importance Islam attaches to such values as mercy and compassion. One of God's names, according to the Qur'an, is *as-salam*, which means peace. Moreover the Qur'an states that the Prophet Muhammad ﷺ was sent to the world as a mercy to mankind. (21:107)

A perusal of the Qur'an shows that most verses of the Qur'an (and also the *Hadith*) are based on peace and kindness, either directly or indirectly. The ideal society, according to the Qur'an is *Dar as-Salam*, that is, the house of peace (10:25).

The Qur'an presents the universe as a model which is characterised by harmony and peace (36:40) When God created heaven and earth, He so ordered things that each part might perform its function peacefully without clashing with any other part. The Qur'an tells us that "the sun is not allowed to overtake the moon, nor does the night outpace the day. Each in its own orbit runs." (36:40)

For billions of years, therefore, the entire universe has been fulfilling its function in total harmony with His divine plan.

These are only but a few references to show what great importance Islam attaches to peace. In fact, Islam cannot afford not to be in a state of peace because all that Islam aims at—spiritual progress, intellectual development, character building, social reform, educational activities, and above all *da'wah*—can be achieved only in an atmosphere of peace and harmony.

According to Islam, peace is not simply an absence of war. Peace opens doors to all kinds of opportunities which are present in any given situation. It is only in a peaceful situation that planned activities are possible. It is for this reason that the Qur'an says 'reconciliation is the best' (4:128) Similarly the Prophet Muhammad ﷺ has observed: "God grants to gentleness (*rifq*) what he does not grant to violence (*unf*). (Sunan Abu Dawud 4/255).

Some people bracket justice with peace, but Islam does not subscribe to this notion. Islam believes in peace for the sake of peace. According to Islam, justice is not the direct result of peace. Peace only provides a framework within which we may work towards justice. There are so many examples in the life of the Prophet which prove that Prophet never bracketed justice with peace.

He always took peaceful circumstances as an opportunity to work for justice and did not attempt to derive justice directly from peace. One such clear example is provided by the treaty of Hudaybiyya, between the Prophet and his opponents. From the details of the peace treaty it is clear that no clause regarding justice was included. Obviously the conditions of this treaty was quite against justice. But the Prophet accepted this treaty, not because it was giving them justice, but because it was *paving the way to work for justice.*

Because of the importance of peace, the Qur'an has clearly declared that no aggressive war is permitted in Islam. Muslims can engage themselves only in a defensive, not in an offensive war, irrespective of the circumstances (2:190)

According to Islam, peace is the rule and war is only an exception. Even in defensive war we have to see the result. If the result is doubtful, Muslims should avoid war, even in a defensive situation. Stray acts of aggression are not enough for Muslims to rush into war. They have to assess the whole situation and adopt a policy of avoidance when war is not certain to achieve a positive result.

There are several examples of this kind in the early period of Islam. In Islamic history, one such example is that of the battle of the trench. In this event there was clear-cut aggression on the part of the antagonists, who travelled as far as 300 miles from Makkah to Madinah only to attack the Muslims. But the Prophet dug a trench in order to prevent an armed confrontation and thus avoided engaging in a defensive war.

It is true that *jihad* is one of the most important teachings of Islam. But *jihad* is not synonymous with war. In Islam another word is used for war and fighting. This word is *'qital.'* When the Qur'an refers to war or fighting, it uses the word *qital* and not *jihad*.

Jihad literally means to strive or to struggle. So *jihad* actually means peaceful struggle, especially for *da'wah* work. The Qur'an says: Do great *jihad* with the help of the Qur'an. (25:52)

The Qur'an is simply a book, and not a sword, "so do great jihad with the Qur'an" means 'do great *jihad* with the ideological power of the Qur'an. In fact, *jihad* is only another name for peaceful activism. And peaceful activism is the only weapon by which Islam wants to achieve all its aims and objectives.

The Qur'an has this to say of the mission of the Prophet Muhammad ﷺ: We have not sent you forth but as a mercy to mankind. (21:107)

In the Qur'an and the *Hadith*, there are many such references which go to prove that Islam is a religion of peace, love and human brotherhood. However, it is also a fact that in later times the image of Islam has altered drastically. Now Islam has come to be regarded as a religion of violence rather than as a religion of peace. This transformation in the image of Islam has not simply been produced by the media. The responsibility for this falls on latter-day Muslims, who have failed to maintain the original image of Islam.

In actual fact, the mission of all the prophets right from

Adam to Christ was one and the same—of establishing the ideology of monotheism in the world, so that man might worship one God alone. As we know, there came a large number of prophets in ancient times, but the message of monotheism remained at the initial stage; it could not culminate in revolution. This state continued up till the time of Christ, the last but one Prophet. The reason being that in ancient times, the system of monarchy was entrenched throughout the world. The kings, in order to secure their political interests, adopted the course of religious persecution. These kings suppressed all religious movements, which were different from the state religion. They would nip all apostasy in the bud, since they saw religion as a matter of affirming one's loyalty to the state. If a person adhered to a religion other than the state religion, he was regarded as a rebel.

That is why in ancient times prophetic movements could go no further ahead than the stage of *da'wah*. No sooner would a movement based on monotheism arise than the coercive political system would be activated to pull it out by its roots. The reason for the absence of any historical record of prophets (besides the Prophet Muhammadﷺ) in antiquity is traceable to the intense opposition of these coercive political systems. All the Prophets of ancient times, historically speaking, were like mythical beings, rather than real human beings accepted as historical figures. The Prophet Jesus was the last link in the chain of these persecutions faced by the preachers of monotheism. Then God decreed the abolition of this coercive political system, even if it entailed the use of force in order that the age of religious persecution might be brought to an end forever , and replaced by the age of religious freedom. This divine plan was brought to completion through the Prophet Muhammad ﷺ and his companions. This is the command given in the Qur'an:

> Fight them until there be no persecution and religion be wholly Allah's (8:39).

Therefore the Prophet Muhammad ﷺ received special divine succour in the form of a powerful team consisting of one hundred thousand individuals. Equipped with this team the Prophet waged war to end this coercive system of religious persecution, and it was in Arabia that it was first of all overthrown. Then within a very short span of time, they advanced to abolish the coercive system established by the Sassanid and Byzantine empires. In the wake of this Islamic action, the coercive system was abolished forever in the major part of the inhabited world of the time. This war waged by the Prophet Muhammad ﷺ and his companions was not a war as is commonly understood, but rather a divine operation, which was carried out by a people who possessed a high standard of moral character.

However, this operation was certainly only temporary in nature. Its goal was to put an end to the age of religious persecution and usher in the age of religious freedom. This end was fully achieved during the early period of Islam, the age of the pious Caliphs. Afterwards the time came to keep the sword in its sheath and engage in *da'wah* work, that is, the call to God, which was the real and permanent goal of Islam. According to the explicit command of the Qur'an, the call to God is the true and eternal mission of

Islam, whereas war is only temporary and allowed only in exceptional cases.

Here it would be pertinent to refer to a great companion of the Prophet. After the period of the pious Caliphate, a group of Muslims once again engaged in war. At that time some senior Companions were present in Makkah and Madinah. But they did not join these wars, one prominent name being that of Abdullah ibn Umar ibn Khattab. He did not approve of these wars, therefore he remained away from them. Some of those involved in these wars came to him and said: God has commanded us in the Qur'an to fight against *fitna* (persecuation). Then why do you not join with us in these wars? Abdullah ibn Umar replied that "the command of the Qur'an to fight against *fitna* is not what you hold to be *fitna*. *Fitna* meant religious persecution and we have already fought and put an end to this *fitna (qad fa'alna)*. Therefore now after the removal of this obstacle, we have to engage ourselves in peaceful *da'wah* work, rather than initiating hostilities and creating new *fitna* once again, which is akin to creating new obstacles for peaceful Islamic *da'wah* (al-Bukhari, Sahih, *Kitab at-Tafsir*, under *al-Baqarah* and *al-Anfal*).

Abdullah ibn Umar had made an extremely pertinent point at the most appropriate time, but this point of view was not forcefully taken up by others. Afterwards when the Islamic sciences were developed, this important point made by Abdullah ibn Umar could not be highlighted, with the result that history took the course of wars and conquests, while in terms of the real teachings of Islam, history should have taken the course of *da'wah* and the propagation of Islam.

It is no exaggeration to say that Islam and violence are contradictory to each other. The concept of Islamic violence is so obviously unfounded that, prima facie it stands rejected. The fact that violence is not sustainable in the present world is enough to convince one that violence as a principle is quite alien to the scheme of things in Islam. Islam claims to be an eternal religion and such a religion cannot afford a principle in its scheme which will not be sustainable in later periods of human history. An attempt to bracket violence with Islam amounts to casting doubts upon the very eternity of the Islamic religion.

No wonder, then, that the Prophet Muhammad ﷺ so earnestly used to entreat his Lord in his daily prayer: "O God, you are the original source of Peace; from You is all Peace, and to You returns all Peace. So, make us live with Peace; and let us enter paradise: the House of Peace. Blessed be You, our Lord, to whom belongs all Majesty and Honour!"

11

❦

Non-Violence and Islam

Non-violence should never be confused with inaction or passivity. Non-violence is action in the full sense of the word. Rather it is more forceful an action than that of violence. It is a fact that non-violent activism is more powerful and effective than violent activism. Non-violent activism is not limited in its sphere. It is a course of action which may be followed in all matters.

Whenever individuals, groups or communities are faced with a problem, one way to solve it is by resorting to violence. The better way is to attempt to solve the problem by peaceful means, avoiding violence and confrontation. Peaceful means may take various forms. In fact, it is the nature of the problem which will determine which of these peaceful methods is applicable to the given situation.

Islam is a religion which teaches non-violence. According to the Qur'an, God does not love *fasad*, violence. What is meant here by fasad is clearly expressed in verse 205 of the second chapter. Basically, *fasad* is that action which results in disruption of the social system, causing huge losses in terms of lives and property.

Conversely, we can say with certainty that God loves nonviolence. He abhors violent activity being indulged in human society, as a result of which people have to pay the price with their possessions and lives. This is supported by other statements in the Qur'an. For instance, we are told in the Qur'an that peace is one of God's names (59:23). Those who seek to please God are assured by verse 5 of the sixteenth *surah* that they will be guided by Him to "the paths of peace." Paradise, which is the final destination of the society of God's choice, is referred to in the Qur'an as "the home of peace" (89:30), etc.

The entire spirit of the Qur'an is in consonance with this concept. For instance, the Qur'an attaches great importance to patience. In fact, patience is set above all other Islamic virtues with the exceptional promise of reward beyond measure. (39:10)

Patience implies a peaceful response or reaction, whereas impatience implies a violent response. The word sabr exactly expresses the notion of nonviolence as it is understood in modern times. That patient action is nonviolent action has been clearly expressed in the Qur'an. According to one tradition, the Prophet Muhammad ﷺ observed: God grants to *rifq* (gentleness) what he does not grant to *unf* (violence). (Abu Dawud, *Sunan*, 4/255)

The word *rifq* has been used in this *hadith* as an antithesis to *unf*. These terms convey exactly what is meant by violence and nonviolence in present times. This *hadith* clearly indicates the superiority of the nonviolent method.

God grants to nonviolence what He does not grant to

violence is no simple matter. It has very wide and deep implications. It embodies an eternal law of nature. By the very law of nature all bad things are associated with violence, while all good things are associated with nonviolence.

Violent activities breed hatred in society, while nonviolent activities elicit love. Violence is the way of destruction while nonviolence is the way of construction. In an atmosphere of violence, it is enmity which flourishes, while in an atmosphere of nonviolence, it is friendship which flourishes. The method of violence gives way to negative values while the method of nonviolence is marked by positive values. The method of violence embroils people in problems, while the method of nonviolence leads people to the exploiting of opportunities. In short, violence is death, nonviolence is life.

Both the Qur'an and the *Hadith* have attached great importance to *jihad*. What is *jihad*? Jihad means struggle, to struggle one's utmost. It must be appreciated at the outset that this word is used for nonviolent struggle as opposed to violent struggle. One clear proof of this is the verse of the Qur'an (25:52) which says: Perform *jihad* with this (i.e. the words of the Qur'an) most strenuously.

The Qur'an is not a sword or a gun. It is a book of ideology. In such a case performing *jihad* with the Qur'an would mean an ideological struggle to conquer peoples' hearts and minds through Islam's superior philosophy.

In the light of this verse of the Qur'an, *jihad* in actual fact is another name for peaceful activism or nonviolent activism. Where *qital* is violent activism, *jihad* is nonviolent activism.

Peaceful Beginning

When the Qur'an began to be revealed, the first verse of the revelation conveyed the injunction: 'Read!' (Iqra) (96:1). By perusing this verse we learn about the initiation of Islamic action. It begins from the point where there is hope of continuing the movement along peaceful lines, and not from that point where there are chances of its being marred by violence.

When the command of *'iqra'* was revealed, there were many options available in Makkah as starting points for a movement. For instance, one possible starting point was to launch a movement to purify the Kabah of the 360 idols installed in it. But, by pursuing such a course, the Islamic movement at that juncture would certainly have had to face a violent reaction from the Quraysh. An alternative starting point could have been an attempt to secure a seat in the Dar-al-Nadwa (Makkah's parliament). At that time almost the whole of Arabia was under the direct or indirect influence of the Roman and Sasanid empires. If the freeing of Arabia from this influence had been made the starting point, this would also have been met with an immediate violent reaction on the part of the Quraysh.

Leaving aside these options, the path followed was that of reading the Qur'an, an activity that could be, with certainty, continued along peaceful lines: no violent reaction would ensue from engaging in such an activity.

The Prophet Muhammad ﷺ followed this principle throughout his life. His policy was that of adopting non-violent methods in preference to violent methods. It is this policy which was referred to by Aishah, the Prophet's wife, in these words: Whenever the Prophet had to opt for one of two ways, he almost always opted for the easier one. (*Fath al-Bari*, 6/654)

What are the advantages of non-violent activism over violent activism? They are briefly stated as under:

1. According to the Qur'an there are two faculties in every human being which are mutually antipathetic. One is the ego, and the other is the conscience called respectively *nafs ammara* and *nafs lawwama*. (The Qur'an, 12:53; 75:26) What the violent method invariably does is to awaken the ego which necessarily results in a breakdown of social equilibrium. On the other hand, non-violent activism awakens the conscience. From this results an awakening in people of introspection and self-appraisal. And according to the Qur'an, the miraculous outcome of this is that "he who is your enemy will become your dearest friend." (41:34)

2. A great advantage of the non-violent method is that, by following it, no part of one's time is wasted. The opportunities available in any given situation may then be exploited to the fullest extent—as happened after the no-war pact of Hudaybiyya. This peace treaty enabled the energies of the believers to be utilised in peaceful constructive activities instead of being dissipated in a futile armed encounter. One great harm done by violent activism is the breaking of social traditions in the launching of militant movements. Conversely, the great benefit that accrues from non-violent activism is that it can be initiated and prolonged with no damage to tradition.

Generally speaking, attempts to improve or replace existing systems by violent activism are counter-productive.

One coup d'état is often the signal for a series of coups and counter-coups. The truly desirable revolution is that which permits gradual and beneficial changes. And this can be achieved only on the basis of non-violence.

Success Through the Non-violent Method

All the great successes of the first phase of Islam as well as the succeeding periods were achieved by non-violent methods. Listed below are some examples of these successes.

1. Of the 23 year period of prophethood, the initial 13 years were spent by the Prophet in Makkah. The Prophet fully adopted the way of pacifism or non-violence during this time. There were many such issues in Makkah at that time which could have been the subject of clash and confrontation. But, sedulously avoiding all such issues, the Prophet Muhammad ﷺ strictly limited his sphere to peaceful propagation of the word of God. This resulted in *da'wah* work being performed in full force throughout this period. One of the great gains during these 13 years of *da'wah* work was the entry into the Islamic fold of men of the highest moral calibre, who were responsible for forming the history of Islam, for instance, Abu Bakr, Umar, Uthman and Ali, etc.

2. In Makkah when the Quraysh leaders were set to wage war against the Prophet, even then, instead of opting for the way of reaction and retaliation, what the Prophet did was to secretly migrate to Madinah.

   Migration, by its very nature, was a clear example of non-violent activism. This peaceful strategy enabled the Prophet and his followers, about two hundred in number, to form a powerful centre of Islam in Madinah. Had they adopted the path of confrontation instead of peaceful migration, the history of Islam might have been buried right there in Makkah shortly after its inception.

3. After the emigration, his antagonists took the unilateral decision to wage war against him. Consequently such bloody encounters as those of Badr and Uhud took place. Then the Prophet made a 10-year peace treaty known in history as Sulh al-Hudaybiyya, by accepting all the conditions of his opponents. This has been called a 'clear victory' in the Qur'an. It is this peace treaty, paving the way for peaceful constructive activities which ultimately made possible the conquest of Makkah and the whole of Arabia.

4. By the end of the pious caliphate, a bloody encounter took place between the Banu Hashim and the Banu Umayyah. This stopped the advance of Islam for a period of ten years. What set this process in motion once again was the voluntary withdrawal of Hasan ibn Ali (d. 50 A.H.) from the battlefield. This was undeniably a practical form of non-violent activism. This peaceful move on the part of Hasan ibn Ali re-opened to Islam the locked doors of progress.

5. During the last days of the Abbasid caliphate Mongol tribes attacked the Muslim world and right from Samarkand to Aleppo destroyed the entire Muslim world. The history of Islam had apparently come to a standstill. At that moment the spirit of *da'wah* work was born within the Muslims. As a result, the majority

of the Mongols converted to Islam. And that miracle took place which has been described by an orientalist in these words: "The religion of Muslims has conquered where their arms had failed."

6. Islamic history took a crucial turn when, in the years succeeding the pious caliphate, rot had set in in the system of the government, and the caliphate had turned into monarchy. At that juncture, many factors emerged which would have resulted in clash and confrontation between the ruler and the ruled. But, following the guidance of the Prophet, the Muslims totally avoided political confrontation. This history beginning with the Umayyad caliphate, continued for several centuries. This was possible because the *tabi'un* (companions of the Prophet's companions) and their succeeding generations, consisting of traditionists, jurists, *'ulama,* sufis and other great religious scholars, all scrupulously avoided any clash or confrontation with the rulers.

It was during this period that on the one hand peaceful *da'wah* work was started in various countries while on the other, disciplines of *hadith, fiqh* and other Islamic sciences came into existence on a large scale after a long period of great struggle. All the precious books which adorn our libraries, all the classical literature of Islam are the result of these peaceful activities.

For instance, the Hadith as a source of *Shari'ah is* second only to the Qur'an in Islam. These traditions now exist in the form of printed books. These books are so precious that, without them, it would not have been possible to develop Islam into a complete system as it exists today. During the

Umayyads and Abbasids, when the political system had begun to deteriorate, where were these tens of thousands of traditions. All of them existed in the memory of the religious scholars, whose names are mentioned in the books as chains in the link of authorities who have handed this legacy down to us. Had they adopted the principle of violent activism and clashed with the 'oppressive' rulers, they would all have been slaughtered by them and the entire legacy of traditions, instead of finding a place on the pages of books, would have been buried along with them in the graveyards. It is by the miracle of having adopted non-violence instead of violence that the precious sources of traditions have survived in book form and, till today, adorn our libraries.

Political Revolt Unlawful

Despite the blatant perversion in the Muslim rulers after the pious caliphate, the Muslim ulema did not lead an insurrection against these corrupt individuals. For about a period of one thousand years they remained detached in this matter and continued to engage all their efforts in non-political fields. This was not a matter of accident but in obedience to the express injunctions of the shariah.

As we know, in the books of *Hadith* detailed traditions have been set down in the chapters titled *Kitab al-Fitan*. The Prophet Muhammad ﷺ observed in plain words that in later times perversions would set in in the rulers, they would become tyrannical and unjust, but that Muslims should not wield their swords against them. They should rather move to the mountains with their goats and camels.

By 'goats and camels' are meant the opportunities in non-political fields which exist, even when the political institutions are corrupted. This injunction given by the Prophet meant that the Muslims should avail of such opportunities by avoiding clash and confrontation in the political field. In short, by ignoring the political problem, they should avail of the non-political opportunities.

These injunctions of the Prophet Muhammad ﷺ were so clear that the Muslim ulema of later times formed a consensus to make insurrection against the rulers unlawful.

Imam An-Nawawi, commenting upon some traditions as set forth by *Sahih* Muslim (*Kitab al-Imarah*) observes: "You should not come into conflict with the rulers in matters of their power. Even if you find them going against express Islamic injunctions, you should attempt to make the truth clear to them solely through words of wisdom and advice. So far as revolt and war against them in order to unseat them is concerned, that is totally unlawful according to the consensus of the ulema, even when the rulers are *zalim* and *fasiq* (tyrants and corrupt)." (*Sahih Muslim, bi sharh an-Nawawi*, 12/229)

This command of the Prophet, as clearly expressed above, was based on extremely important considerations. In actual fact, in the early phase of Islam (as well as in the later phase) *da'wah* and reform works had to be performed, without which the history of Islam would not have been complete. If the ulema of the Muslim community had tried to pose a threat to the political institutions, certainly all this constructive work would have been left undone. That is why the Prophet Muhammad ﷺ expressly prohibited any clash with political institutions. This avoidance of strife guaranteed that non-political constructive work would continue to be performed without any break.

In every society there are always two systems side by side, one political and the other non-political. The latter is established through various non-political institutions. According to the scheme of Islam, non-political institutions established at the social level have always to remain stable. In this way there is a continuing endeavour—even when the political institutions have become corrupt, or keep changing—to keep Islam firmly established at the level of the non-political system.

The Command of War in Islam

It is a fact that certain verses in the Qur'an convey the command to do battle (*qital*) (22:39). What the special circumstances are which justify the issuance of and compliance with this command we learn from our study of the Qur'an.

1.   The first point to be noted is that aggression or the launching of an offensive by the believers is not totally forbidden. It is permissible, but with certain provisos. We are clearly commanded in the Qur'an: Fight for the sake of God those that fight against you, *but do not be aggressive.* (2:190)

2.   Only defensive war is permitted in Islam. Such a war is one in which aggression is committed by some other party so that the believers have to fight in self-defence. Initiating hostility is not permitted for Muslims. The Qur'an says: "They were the first to attack you." (9:13) Furthermore, even in the case of the offensive being

launched by an opposing group, the believers are not supposed to retaliate immediately. Rather in the beginning all efforts are to be made to avert war, and only when avoidance has become impossible is battle to be resorted to inevitably in defence.

3. According to the Qur'an there was one form of war which was time-bound strictly in relation to its purpose. This was to put an end to *fitna*. 'Fight against them until *fitna* is no more.' (2:193) In this verse *fitna* signifies that coercive system which had reached the extremes of religious persecution. In ancient times this coercive political system prevailed all over the world. This absolutism had closed all the doors of progress, both spiritual and material. At that time God commanded the believers to break this coercive system in order to usher in freedom, so that all doors of spiritual and material progress might be opened to man.

This mission was undertaken and brought to a successful conclusion at the internal level within Arabia during the life of the Prophet. Later, during the pious caliphate, the Sassanid and Byzantine empires were dismantled with special divine succour. Consequently, intellectual oppression at the international level was replaced by intellectual freedom.

In this connection those traditions are worth noting which are enshrined in *Sahih al-Bukhari*. When, after the fourth caliph Ali ibn Abi Talib, political conflict ensued between Abdullah ibn Zubayr and the Umayyads, Abdullah ibn Umar, one of the seniormost companions of the Prophet held himself aloof from the battle. People approached him and, quoting the verse of *qital-al-fitna*, asked him why he was not joining in the battle. Abdullah ibn Umar replied that *'fitna'* as mentioned in the Qur'an did not refer to political infighting, but rather to the religious coercive system, that had already been put to an end by them. (*Fathul Bari*, 8/60)

From this we learn that the war against *fitna* was a war of limited duration, temporary in nature, meant to be engaged in only until its specific purpose had been served.

Invoking the Qur'anic exhortation to do battle against *fitna* in order to validate acts of war which had quite other aims is highly improper. This verse could be cited only if the same state of affairs as existed at the time of its revelation, were to prevail once again.

The biographers of the Prophet Muhammad ﷺ have put the number of *ghazwa* (battle) at more than 80. This gives the impression that the Prophet Muhammad ﷺ in his 23-year prophetic career waged about four battles in a year. But this impression is entirely baseless. The truth is that the Prophet Muhammad ﷺ in his entire prophetic life, engaged in war only on three occasions. All the other incidents described as *ghazwat* were in actual fact examples of avoidance of war and not instances of involvement in battle.

For instance, in the books of *Seerah*, the incident of Al-Ahzab is called a *ghazwa* (battle), whereas the truth is that on this occasion the armed tribes of Arabia, twelve thousand in number, reached the borders of Madinah with all intentions of waging war, but the Prophet and his companions dug a deep trench between them, thus successfully preventing a battle from taking place. The same is the case with all the other incidents called *ghazwa*. The opponents of the Prophet repeatedly tried to get him embroiled in war, but on all such occasions, he managed to resort to some such strategy as averted the war, thus defusing the situation.

There were only three instances of Muslims really entering the field of battle—Badr, Uhud and Hunayn. But the events tell us that on all these occasions, war had become inevitable, so that the Prophet was compelled to encounter the aggressors in self-defence. Furthermore, these battles lasted only for half a day, each beginning from noon and ending with the setting of the sun. Thus it would be proper to say that the Prophet in his entire life span had actively engaged in war for a total of a day and a half. That is to say, the Prophet had observed the principle of non-violence throughout his 23-year prophetic career, except for one and a half days.

The Islamic method, being based totally on the principle of non-violence, it is unlawful for believers to initiate hostilities. Except in cases where self-defence has become inevitable, the Qur'an in no circumstance gives permission for violence.

The Modern Age and Non-Violence

The greatest problem facing Islam today is, as I see it, that Muslims have almost totally forgotten the sunnah (Prophet's way) of non-violence. In later times when the Ottoman and Mughal empires disintegrated and problems like that of Palestine have had to be confronted by the faithfuls, Muslims all over the world have fallen a prey to negative reaction on a colossal scale; they have failed to remember that the policy of Islam is not that of violence but of nonviolence. It is the result of this deviation, that despite almost a 100-years of bloody wars, Muslims have achieved no positive gain. Rather whatever they already had has been lost by them.

According to Imam Malik, later generations of this ummah (Muslim community) will be able to settle matters at issue in the same way that earlier generations had done, i.e. non-violent methods. Similarly, Muslims of modern times must likewise resort only to non-violent methods. Just as no gain could accrue from violent methods earlier, no gain can accrue from violent methods today.

The state of affairs of Muslims in modern times resembles that which prevailed at the time of Hudaybiyya. Today once again—only on a far larger scale—this *hamiyat al-jahiliya*, prejudices prevailing in pre-Islamic Arabia (48:28) is being displayed by the other party. In the first phase of Islam its solution lay in Muslims sedulously avoiding an equivalent display of prejudice, and in holding firmly *kalima at-taqwa* (the word of piety) they became entitled to the succour of God and were granted a clear victory (48:26).

At the time of the Hudaybiyya peace treaty, the Quraysh, who had secured the leadership of Arabia, were bent on waging war. The Kabah was in their possession. They had expelled the Prophet and his companions from their home-town. They had taken possession of Muslims' homes and other properties, and spared no effort in disseminating negative propaganda against Islam.

Given this state of affairs, there were only two options before the believers. One was to attempt to put an end to tyranny and launch an outright war on the other party in the name of securing their rights. The result of such a move would certainly have been further loss in terms of lives and property.

The second option was to remain patient in the face of immediate loss, be it political or material, and, in spite of the losses avail of whatever opportunities are already available. The Prophet Muhammad 🌺 and his companions chose this second course. The result was that the entire history of Arabia was revolutionized in just a few years time.

The same state of affairs is widespread in modern times. Although today Muslims have suffered great losses, political and material, at the hands of other nations, however there still exist a great number of opportunities on a far larger scale. If availed of wisely, we can rewrite the history of Islam in magnificent terms.

The Manifestation of Religion

The modern age is regarded by Muslims as being fraught with problems for Islam. But this is quite contrary to the actual situation. The modern age was in fact the age of Islam, just as the period of rainfall is the period of farmers. But Muslims, lacking in understanding and awareness have failed to understand this; hence their failure to convert this potential into reality.

What is called *izhar ad-din* in the Qur'an does not refer to something which is temporary in nature. It, in fact, refers to an eternal ideological ascendancy of Islam. It means that in the world of ideology, such a revolution would be brought about as would establish the ideological supremacy of Islam forever. God has already brought it into existence potentially, the believers have only to tap and convert this potential into reality.

The aim of the revolution brought about by the

Prophet and his companions in the seventh century is stated to be *izhar ad-din* in the Qur'an:

> 'They desire to extinguish the light of Allah with their mouths: but Allah seeks only to perfect His light, however much the infidels may abhore it (9:32-33).

Izhar in Arabic means dominance / ascendancy / supremacy. Here *izhar ad-din* signifies intellectual and ideological dominance, not political dominance. This means that in intellectual and ideological respect, God's religion assumes ascendancy over all other ideologies and religions for all time.

Granting ideological ascendancy to God's religion was no simple matter. It amounted to the writing of history afresh. For although God's religion had always been in a superior position ideologically, it had become obscured by false and misguided ideas. The reason being that in ancient times people were heavily under the influence of superstitious thinking. Their arts and learning in general had all become fettered by superstition and idolatry. This had led to a veil being thrown over true religion, which was the only vehicle for God's truth.

God desired that through the final Prophet an intellectual revolution be brought about which would alter this unfavourable and artificial state of affairs. That human sciences themselves become supporters of the true religion so that according to the established academic standard itself, the religion of monotheism may be made an established religion for the people.

By *izhar ad-din* in this verse is meant this same divine plan being brought into a revolution by the Prophet and his companions. This revolution set a new process in human history. Its purpose was to unravel all the veils of superstition which clouded human judgement, and to lay bare the scientific proofs hidden in nature, so that the truth of monotheism could be brought to light for all humanity. In modern times this revolution has reached its culmination. There were two main aims of this *izhar ad-din*. One, that the system of religious persecution be put to an end, so that a propitious atmosphere could be created for the performance of *da'wah* of the true religion. In ancient times this task could only be performed in a very adverse atmosphere. The second purpose was to rally all arguments in support of God's true religion, so that all other religions might be shown to be totally lacking in the sound base of arguments. Both these tasks have been performed on a large scale in present times. A brief mention of these is made here.

In ancient times the monarchical system prevailed all over the world. And individualistic system like monarchy could be established by force alone. That is why a coercive system of governance was established by the monarchs. They inevitably crushed any sign of intellectual or religious freedom found among their subjects. This state of affairs posed a permanent obstacle to the general development of human thought or to the spreading of any religious mission. Ultimately this coercive political system was destroyed by the revolution brought about by the Prophet and his Companions.

This abolition of oppressive systems and the freeing of peoples' minds from superstition ushered in an era of freedom and democracy. The effect of this revolution in human history set in motion a process. Later on western nations contributed greatly towards this revolution in human thought. Now this process has culminated in the unparalleled scientific achievements of the present day. In consequence, it has become possible for the task of *da'wah* of truth to be performed in an atmosphere of freedom, which was earlier seriously hampered by the oppressive atmosphere.

Idolatry is another name for a religion of superstitions. In ancient times this *shirk* (idolatry) dominated the minds of the people, having rendered the progress and development of science impossible. The Prophet and his companions made great sacrifices to put an end to this superstitious system. In this way the age of science had its beginnings. The changes wrought by it influenced the course of history over the centuries.*

The scientific revolution, which was in actual fact a by-product of the Islamic revolution, gave us modern communications. The advent of this new age made it possible for the first time in human history for the propagation of Islam to be carried out on a universal scale. According to a *hadith* a time was to come when God's words would enter all the homes in the world. (*Musnad*, Ahmad) This was indirectly, a prediction of the modern age of communications.

One outcome of the modern scientific revolution is that we have at our disposal a number of new arguments in support of Islamic beliefs. Prior to this revolution the *da'is* of Islam could resort only to traditional arguments in support of the truth of Islam. But today it has become

---

* For detail, see *Islam the Creator of the Modern Age* by the author.

possible to measure up Islamic realities by the highest standards of human knowledge and to establish its authenticity by purely logical arguments.

In ancient times the study of religion could be done only as something sacred and as a matter of dogma. That is why established and unestablished religions had not academically been distinguished from one another. In modern times, owing to the influence of the scientific revolution the study of religions can be done as objectively and as critically as any other matter which comes under scientific scrutiny.

Such critical study has proved, purely academically, that by historical standards, there is only one reliable religion, and that is Islam. All other religions are lacking in this historical credibility. After this intellectual revolution it has become possible to establish the truth of Islam vis-a-vis other religions purely on the basis of human knowledge. That Islam is the only authentic version of divine religion may be fully supported by arguments.

These modern development in our times have taken Islam to the point of unopposed victory. Now the need of the hour is for Muslims to put an end unilaterally to all violent activities against *mad'u* nations, so that a normal relationship may be allowed to grow between *da'i* and *mad'u*, only then the message of Islam can be conveyed in a normal situation. Now, in the wake of the scientific revolution it has become possible to begin a serious and beneficial dialogue between Islam and non-Islam, the result of which will necessary be in favour of Islam.

A Great Opportunity

1. Since direct argument cannot be applied to religious beliefs pertaining to the unseen world, these can be

supported only by indirect or inferential argument. Educated people had therefore come to believe that religious realities belonged only to the domain of dogma, and that they were not academic or scientific realities. But after the breaking up of the atom the science of logic has undergone a change, and it has been accepted that inferential argument too, in its nature, is as valid and reliable as direct argument. It has subsequently become possible for religious realities to be established on an academic level, i.e. exactly on the same level as material or non-religious theories.*

2. In ancient times when man observed the world, it appeared to him that in nature there existed things which were very different from one another. This observation of appearance produced the mentality of idolatry. People began to think that in view of the great diversity of things in existence, their Creator too ought to be more than one. But scientific study has shown that this variety is only that of appearance. Otherwise, all things in nature are different expressions of the same matter. In this way *shirk* (idolatry) lost its intellectual base while monotheism gained the solid support of logic.

3. According to a statement of the Qur'an, the signs of God lay hidden in the earth and the heavens. The study of science has made it manifest to all that the universe is a great storehouse of divine arguments. "We will show them Our signs in all the regions of the earth and

---

*   For detail, refer to *Religion and Science* by the author.

in their own souls, until they clearly see that this is the Truth." (41:53)

4.   After the new discoveries of science, many such things have come to the knowledge of man as have rendered it possible to prove with new arguments those events which are of important religious significance. For instance, carbon-dating has made it possible to determine the exact age of the mummy of Rameses II, thereby providing scientific proof for the statement of the Qur'an that the body of Pharaoh was saved by God, so that it might become "a sign to all posterity." (10:92)

♦ Islam in the Present Age

Now the question arises as to whether an Islam which teaches non-violence can be of relevance in the present age, and assume a superior position once again in new situations.

The answer is entirely in the positive. The truth is that Islam's being a peaceful religion shows that it is an eternal religion. Had it been a religion of violence, it would not have been eternal. For, in modern times, the way of violence has been totally rejected by contemporary thinking. Now only that system is worthy of consideration and acceptance the teachings of which are based on peace and non-violence.

Modern thinking, for example, has rejected communism. One of the major reasons was that communism had to be sustained by violence. And under no circumstances is violence acceptable to the modern mind. Nazism and Fascism too have been rejected on similar grounds. Modern man, therefore, disapproves of both religious and non-religious extremism, because they lead man ultimately to violence.

But Islam is a religion of nature. It has held violence as inadmissible from the outset. Islam has been an upholder of peace, not violence, from day one.

In the past, Islam played a great role in the development of humanity, as a result of which human history entered a new age of progress and development. The time has come today for Islam to play a great constructive role, leading human history once again into a new age of progress.

What is called scientific or technical progress is the result of the discovery of some of the great secrets of nature. But if nature and its mysteries have always existed in our world, why has there been such a long delay in their discovery? Why could not the scientific advancement of the last few hundred years have been made thousands of years ago?

The reason was that in ancient times religion and science (divine knowledge and human knowledge) were linked with one another. Religious persecution had become an insuperable obstacle to the progress of science. Scientific enquiry was anathema to men of religion.

What Islam did was separate religion (which had become, in essence, a set of irrational beliefs) from scientific research and investigation. For instance, eclipses of the sun and moon had been linked with human destiny. The Prophet Muhammad ﷺ declared that eclipses had nothing to do with the lot of human beings. These were astronomical events, not events pertaining to the fate of mankind. (*Fathul Bari*, 2/611)

In this connection, an incident of the pollination

of dates is recorded in the books of *Hadith*. The Prophet of Islam observed that in worldly matters such as these, "you should act according to your experience, as you know these matters better." (*Sahih Muslim bi Sharh An-Nawawi*, 15/117)

This meant delinking religion and science from one another. In this way scientific research acquired an atmosphere of freedom for its functioning. For the first time in human history science (human knowledge) could be developed freely without the intervention of religion. And advancing gradually, it culminated in the attainment of the modern age.

But, today man is again facing an even greater problem. That is, despite the extraordinary progress made in the field of science and technology, human beings are confronted with various kinds of problems, without there being any solution in sight. All these problems have resulted from not knowing the limit of freedom.

Modern man aspired to freedom as the highest good, but once having reached this goal, he was unable to set reasonable limits to freedom. In consequence, unrestrained freedom descended into anarchy and lawlessness. This is the actual cause of many of the problems which are emerging in modern times in western society. Now man requires an ideology which delimits his freedom, drawing the line between desirable and undesirable freedom. And it is only Islam which can provide him with such an ideology.

Now is the time for this ideology to be presented to man, who is ready and waiting to accept it. After the fall of communism (1991), the world is faced with an ideological vacuum. This vacuum can be filled by Islam alone. In the present world the developed countries have become economic or military superpowers, but the place is vacant for an ideological superpower, and that, potentially belongs to Islam.

There is only one obstacle in converting a great potential into a reality in favour of Islam. And that is the repeated recourse to violence by Muslim movements in modern times. Such action has presented Islam before the world in the guise of a violent religion. For this reason the man of today shies away from Islam. He fails to study Islam objectively. If this barrier could be removed and Islam once again brought before the world as a non-violent religion, or as a peaceful social system, then once again humanity would accept it, recognising it to be the voice of its own nature.

Modern man is in need of a new religion or a new system, based on peace. It should be free from superstitious beliefs, and should provide the answers to deep psychological questions. Its principles should not clash with scientific realities, and it should be supported by a victorious history.

Today no religion but Islam can lay such positive claims to acceptance, for it is Islam and Islam alone which fulfills all these conditions. Individually, there are many men and women today who, after having studied Islam, have acknowledged these unique qualities in Islam. Some have acknowledged them in theory while others have gone ahead and accepted Islam in practice.

Da'wah Activism

Islamic activism in respect of its method is based on non-violence and in respect of its target is based on *da'wah*. *Da'wah*, in fact, is another name for a peaceful struggle for the propagation of Islam. It would be true to say that Islamic activism in fact is *da'wah* activism.

The task of *da'wah* is no simple one. It enjoys the status of a key factor. If this task is fully performed, all other objectives will be automatically achieved. Here are certain references from the Qur'an in this connection.

1. Through *da'wah* the believers receive God's protection against the mischief of the opponents. (5:67)

2. Through *da'wah* even the direst of enemy turns into a dearest friend. (41:34)

3. *Da'wah* proves Islam's ideological superiority. And without doubt nothing is greater than the superiority of ideology. (10:32)

4. Through *da'wah* a positive mentality is inculcated within the *ummah*. This is called 'honest counsel' in the Qur'an. (7:68)

5. The mission of *da'wah* is performed by human beings but the conducive conditions for it are provided by God. Just as the farming is to be done by the farmer while the rains come from God. In modern times favourable conditions have been fully provided to man. Now the believers' duty is to refrain from expending their energies in futile activities. They must exert their entire energy in *da'wah* work. All the best results will ensue from this act.

6. The Prophet Muhammad ﷺ along with about two hundred of his companions left Makkah when the Makkan leaders had made it impossible for them to stay there. The Makkans had even decided to kill the Prophet. But the first speech the Prophet made on reaching Madinah had no taste of bitterness, neither did it contain any mention of vengeance on or violence against the Quraysh.

On reaching Madinah first priority was given to the task of entering into peace treaties with the tribes in and around Madinah, for instance with the Banu Khuza'a, etc. According to their pact neither would they fight against the Muslims nor would the Muslims fight against them. Most of the tribes in Arabia joined in these truce agreements.

But the Quraysh did not desist from aggression, and even engaged in certain military forays against the Muslims. Finally, in the sixth year of Hijrah, the Prophet succeeded in making a peace treaty with the Quraysh as well at a place called Hudaybiya, albeit on acceptance of all the conditions laid down by the Quraysh.

Muslims Displaced

It is an incontrovertible fact that Muslims have not been able to join the mainstream in modern times. At all places and in every department they are leading their lives as if driven into a corner. This is undoubtedly an extremely critical problem, for it has relegated Muslims to second class positions all over the world.

To me, the greatest reason for this is the violent attitude of the Muslims. Today's Muslims are easily provoked and become violent at anything which is against their way of thinking. It is true that not all Muslims become involved in acts of violence. Yet all Muslims would be regarded involved in this matter. This is because that section of Muslims—in fact, the majority—who are not personally involved, neither disown those members of their community who are engaged in violence, nor even condemn them. In such a case, according to the Islamic shariah itself if the involved Muslims are directly responsible, the uninvolved Muslims are also indirectly responsible.

It is Muslims' religious and secular leaders who are actually responsible for this violent approach on the part of Muslims today. In modern times when Muslims have had to undergo the experience of defeat, almost all the religious and secular scholars as well as intellectuals followed one single line, that of awakening the spirit of *jihad* (in the sense of *qital*) among Muslims. The entire Muslim world reverberated with such slogans as '*jihad* is our way and Jihad is the only solution to our problems!'

The entire world has witnessed a great number of large and small movements in violent response to the problems faced by Muslims. If you go to Palestine, you will hear the youth singing a song, no doubt taught to them by their elders:

> Let's make war, let's make war,
> For war is the way to success.

In modern times the violent approach of our intellectuals, and leaders of movements, is the sole reason for the present violent mentality among Muslims all over the world. It is as a result of this mentality that, if anyone writes a book against Islam, Muslims are prepared to kill the writer. If any procession raises anti-Muslim slogans, Muslims start stoning the procession instead of killing the evil by observing silence, which, as Umar Faruq advocated, would be the best strategy in such a case. If there is any monetary or territorial controversy with any nation, they immediately take up arms against it, rather than adopt a peaceful strategy to solve the problem.

This violent mentality of Muslims is responsible for having alienated them from their neighbours everywhere. Their conduct clearly shows that they no longer cherish the ideal of universal brotherhood. Everywhere they are looked upon with aversion and dread. One can even see notices on walls which say 'Beware of Muslims', instead of 'Beware of dogs.' And if these words are not inscribed on walls, they are certainly inscribed on the hearts and minds of the people. The resulting dissociation has left Muslims a backward group in modern times. Even in advanced countries like America they remain backward as a community in comparison with other immigrant groups.

The only way to alleviate the tragic plight of Muslims is to bring them back to non-violent Islam, by helping them to understand that their violent version of Islam is not the true one.

As soon as Muslims take to the path of non-violent Islam, they will be able to become equal partners with other communities. They will have joined the universal mainstream, and will consequently be able to participate in all activities, in all institutions. People, instead of dreading them, will welcome them in every field. They will become a part of the universal brotherhood. Their issues will be looked upon with justice. Their equal partnership will be certain in all institutions ranging from the social to the educational.

Peaceful interaction will give Muslims the kind of intellectual stimulation and variety of experience which they must have if they are to tread the path of progress. Interaction will also facilitate the task of *da'wah* on a large scale. The natural result of this vast interaction of Muslims and non-Muslims will be that everywhere dialogue on Islam will be started, formally as well as informally. In modern times, because of the extremist and violent attitude of Muslims, serious dialogue between Islam and non-Islam has almost come to an end. Now when peaceful interaction between Muslims and non-Muslims takes place in a normal atmosphere, serious dialogue will ensue on its own. The beginning of serious dialogue between Islam and non-Islam is, without doubt, a very great success from the point of view of *da'wah*.

The Qur'an describes Sulh al-Hudaybiyya, in the early period of Islam as a 'clear victory'. It was a 'clear victory' in the sense that it established peace between the believers in *tawhid* and believers in *shirk*, thus making it possible for a serious dialogue to be held between the two on religious matters.

In modern times if Muslims abandon the path of violence and fully adopt the path of non-violence, this will be for Muslims like reviving the *sunnah* of Hudaybiyya. And they will start receiving those great benefits which Islam and Muslims had gained after the event of Hudaybiya in the first phase.

Peace and Justice

One great problem for Muslims is that peace does not necessarily guarantee them justice. This has caused Muslims to become violent and to neglect opportunities for *da'wah*. In modern times Muslims want a peace which brings them justice. But according to the law of nature, this kind of peace can never be achieved, that is why Muslims the world over are in a state of physical and mental unrest. Distressed in their minds, they have become violent in their thinking and in their actions.

The truth is that peace does not automatically produce justice. Peace in actual fact simply opens up opportunities for the achievement of justice. At the time of Hudaybiyya the Prophet Muhammad ﷺ had not found justice. He had achieved peace but only by delinking it from justice. The Prophet had made this peace not to exact justice but to receive the opportunities. And great opportunities for *da'wah* action did open up with the establishment of peace. The Prophet exploited these opportunities in full measure. Therefore, in just a few years' time the Prophet not only ensured justice, but set Islam upon a much more solid footing.

The Muslims of the present day have to understand this secret of nature. Only then will it be possible for them first to find peace, then ultimately their desired goal of justice.

Conclusion

In October 1997, I met a 36-year old European, Leon Zippo Hayes, who was born in the city of Christchurch in New Zealand. After having studied Islam, he has changed his religion. His Islamic name is Khalilur Rahman. Passing through Muslim countries he is going to perform Hajj by land.

During the conversation he said that in modern times Muslims are engaged in bloody war at many places, at some places with others and at other places among themselves. This had led him (like many others) to conclude that perhaps Islam was a religion of violence. Later, he studied the Qur'an with the help of translations, and when he reached this verse in the Qur'an: 'Whoever killed a human being should be looked upon as though he had killed all mankind (5:32),' he said that he was so moved that he could not believe that it was there in the Qur'an.

This incident is broadly indicative of the thinking of non-Muslims on Islam. On seeing the actions of Muslims, people today find it hard to believe that Islam may be a religion of peace. But if Muslims stop engaging in violent activities and give people the opportunity to appreciate Islam in its original form, then certainly a great number of people would realise as they never had before that Islam was a peaceful religion and they would rush to it, saying that it was exactly the religion which their souls had been seeking all along.

12

⁂❦⁂

Islamic Fundamentalism

Islamic fundamentalism is a recent phenomenon. While studying it we must first of all understand that the term 'Islamic fundamentalism' has not been derived from the Islamic scriptures, nor does any group of Muslims approve of being given the appellation of 'Islamic fundamentalists.' This term is somewhat similar to that of 'Uncle Sam' as applied to Americans by non-Americans. Americans do not identify themselves with this term.

Though this term was given to Muslims by non-Muslims, the phenomenon for which the term Islamic fundamentalism is used is indeed a reality. There is a considerable number of Muslims in the world of today whose thinking and actions add up to what is meant by the term fundamentalism.

That is why a detailed study of its principles and practices must be made in order to evaluate this way of thinking and the movements spawned by it, which are highly active all over the world under one name or another.

Let us first of all find out what is commonly meant by

fundamentalism. I would personally prefer to call this phenomenon 'Islamic extremism,' rather than 'Islamic fundamentalism,' although those engaged in extremist activities would, like the fundamentalists, prefer not to be called extremists. However, what is important in this connection is that the phenomenon of Islamic extremism can be explained from a Quranic verse. It says: "Do not transgress the bounds of your religion (4:17)." One modern form of transgression, as forbidden in the Quran, is what is now called Islamic fundamentalism.

There are certain Muslims who say: "Yes, we are fundamentalists. And what is wrong with being fundamentalists?" They take the word "fundamentalist" in its literal sense of laying emphasis on the basic teachings of Islam. Thus, attaching importance to the basic teachings of Islam is to fulfill the very demand of Islam. So why should anyone have any objection on this score?

But herein lies a fallacy. That is, if one takes fundamentalism in its literal sense, then it should be the same basic teachings of Islam as are emphasized in the Islamic scriptures themselves. This cannot mean that any individual may declare, through personal interpretation, some self-styled teachings to be the basic teachings or the fundamentals of Islam, and then launch a violent movement aimed at establishing these so-called Islamic fundamentals. Unfortunately this is what these fundamentalists are doing.

Now what are the basic teachings of Islam? The principle concern of Islam is monotheism. According to an orientalist, "the central focus of Islam is Allah. That is to believe in one God; associating all one's feelings of love and fear with Him; and worshipping Him alone. Then adhering strictly to justice in one's dealings with other human beings, returning good for evil, and so on.

In Islam, according to a *hadith*, actions are judged by their intentions. That is why Islam lays the greatest of stress on the subjection of human beings to greater and greater degrees of purification. According to a *hadith* the Prophet Muhammad ﷺ observed: "Listen, there is a part made of flesh in the human body. If that is purified and therefore in good order, the whole body is in good order. And if rot sets in in this part, the whole body is defiled. Listen this piece of flesh is the heart." (*Al-Bukhari, Muslim*).

Through this symbol of the body the example of Islamic reform has been expressed. This means that just as through the reform of the heart the human body is reformed, similarly, if a man's thinking and his intentions are virtuous, in respect of his whole existence, he will acquire that character of virtue which is seen as desirable by Islamic standards.

What is Fundamentalism?

Fundamentalism is the laying of emphasis on strict adherence to the fundamental principles of any set of beliefs. The term was originally applied to a particular group of Christian theologians who gained prominence in the United States in the nineteenth Century. They published a series of booklets between 1909 and 1915 called *The Fundamentals: Testimony to the Truth.* In these booklets they defined what they believed to be the absolutely fundamental doctrines of Christianity. The core of these doctrines was the literal inerrancy of every word of the Bible. Those who supported these beliefs during the debate of the 1920s came to be called fundamentalists.

The term "fundamentalism" began to be applied to Islamic resurgence by the final quarter of the twentieth century. However this term was not used for Muslims in exactly the same sense as it was applied to Christians. There is also some difference of opinion on this point among scholars. However, without going into the details of this, I would like to say that the term Islamic fundamentalism is applied to two different kinds of movements. One is like that of the Muslim Brotherhood (*Ikhwanul Muslimun*) which rose to bring about a political revolution. The other is the type which advocates a return to the pristine fundamentals of the faith, for instance, those defined by Ibn Taimiya in the fourteenth century. This latter aim is still the driving force behind the Salafia and Wahabiya movements.

Now the aim of the second form of the Islamic fundamentalism, that of Ibn Taimya is to put an end to additions and innovations (*bid'a*) in religious matters and to replace them with the *sunnah*, the original form of the Islamic Shariah.

The aim of the other form of fundamentalism is to put an end to non-Islamic political set up and replace that with an Islamic political set-up. Both the forms of fundamentalism are totally different from one another. The sphere of the struggle against innovation (*bid'a*) is confined only to matters of belief and worship.

Violence does not, of necessity, accompany movements of this nature. Furthermore, it is aimed at and concerned with the internal reform of Muslims. Thus, in the relevant activities, there is no possibility of coming into conflict with non-Muslims. But so far as fundamentalism of the other kind is concerned, it has been directed from the very outset against political rulers, and whether the inevitable confrontations have been with Muslim or non-Muslim rulers, by its very nature such a movement has demanded the use of violence.

This is where the principle of *jihad* has been distorted and bent to political ends. It must be stressed that the word *"jihad"* has nowhere been used in the Quran to mean the waging of war. The Quran is imbued with the spirit of peace and tolerance. Its culture is not that of war but of mercy.

On Islam and Jihad

At the very beginning of the Qur'an, the first invocation reads: "In the name of God, the most Merciful, the most Beneficent." Throughout the Qur'an, this verse is repeated for no less than 114 times. Even one of God's names is *As-Salam* (Peace). Moreover, the Qur'an states that the Prophet Muhammad ﷺ was sent to the world *as a mercy to mankind* (21:107).

The word 'jihad' has nowhere been used in the Qur'an to mean war in the sense of launching an offensive. It is used rather to mean 'struggle.' The action most consistently called for in the Qur'an is the exercise of patience. Yet today, the 'Muslim Mujahidin' under unfavourable conditions have equated "God is Great" with "War is Great."

In the light of on-going conflict, we must ask why so great a contradiction has arisen between the principles of Islam and the practices of Muslims. At least one root-cause may be traced to historical exigency.

Since time immemorial, military commanders have been accorded positions of great eminence in the annals of history. It is a universal phenomenon that the hero is idolized even in peace time and becomes a model for the people. It is this placing of heroism in the militaristic context which has been the greatest underlying factor in the undue stress laid on war in the latter phase of Islam's history. With the automatic accord in Muslim society of a place of honour and importance to the heroes of the battlefield, annalists' subsequent compilations of Islamic history have tended to read like an uninterrupted series of wars and conquests.

These early chronicles having set the example, subsequent writings on Islamic history have followed the same pattern of emphasis on militarism. The Prophet's biographies were called 'maghazi', that is 'The Battles Fought by the Prophet,' yet the Prophet Muhammad in fact did battle only three times in his entire life, and the period of his involvement in these battles did not total more than one and a half days. He fought, let it be said, in self-defence, when hemmed in by aggressors, where he simply had no option. But historians—flying in the face of fact— have converted his whole life into one of confrontation and war.

We must keep it in mind that the Prophet Muhammad was born at a time when an atmosphere of militancy prevailed in the Arab society. But the Prophet always opted for avoidance of conflict. For instance, in the campaign of Ahzab, the Prophet advised his Companions to dig a trench between them and the enemies, thus preventing a head-on clash.

Another well-known instance of the Prophet's dislike for hostilities is the Hudaibiyyah peace treaty made by accepting, unilaterally, all the conditions of the enemy. In the case of the conquest of Makkah, he avoided a battle altogether by making a rapid entry into the city with ten thousand Muslims—a number large enough to awe his enemies into submission.

In this way, on all occasions, the Prophet endeavoured to achieve his objectives by peaceful rather than by war-like means. It is, therefore, unconscionable that in later biographical writing, all the events of his life have been arranged under the heading of 'battles' (*ghazawat*). How he managed to avert the cataclysms of war has not been dealt with in any of the works which purportedly depict his life.

Ibn Khaldun, the celebrated 14th century historian, was the first to lay down definite rules for the study and writing of history and sociology. He followed the revolutionary course of attempting to present history as a chronicle of events centering on the common man rather than on kings, their generals and the battles they fought. But since war heroes were already entrenched as the idols of society, the caravan of writers and historians continued to follow the same well-worn path as had been trodden prior to Ibn Khaldun. When people have come to regard war heroes as the greatest of men, it is but natural that it is the events of the battlefield which will be given the greatest prominence in works of history. All other events will either be relegated to the background or omitted altogether.

Ideological Hatred

Hatred is a crime and ideological hatred is the greatest crime. The so-called Islamic fundamentalism, if judged by its result, is the greatest crime of this kind against humanity. Any thing can be eliminated, but what is impossible to eliminate is the hatred produced by a sacred ideology: Hatred generates violence and ideological hatred generates unlimited violence. It can kill off all of humanity without suffering any feelings of remorse or repentance. Hence the self-styled Islamic fundamentalism turns into an un-Islamic theory.

One type of movement is that which is based on love. Its aim is to reform human beings. Such a movement awakens in its adherents feelings of well wishing towards other human beings. Its exponents strive peacefully to pass on the truth that they have discovered for the benefit of their fellow men. Such a movement, far from causing harm to society, becomes a driving force towards the moral and social uplift of people in all walks of life.

The other type of movement is one which is based on hatred. The adherents of this movement consider those who are not like-minded to be enemies. They have an overriding desire to wipe them off the face of the earth. They hold that these "enemies" are obstacles to their success and that it is therefore necessary to destroy them altogether. Only then can a system of their own choice be set in place. Islamic fundamentalism—so-called— is a movement of this second type. As a result of this negative thinking they divide humanity into two camps, one consisting of their enemies, and the other of their friends. Once having made this division, they allow their aversion for their "enemies" to grow into virulent hatred. If the incentives for the members of the movement based on love are well-wishing and the goodwill of the people, the incentives for the members of the movement based on hatred are ill-will and animosity. Owing to this negative attitude, all the activities of Islamic fundamentalism take a pernicious direction.

To make matters worse, the hatred felt by the Muslim fundamentalists has become inseparable from their ideology. They hate others who think differently from themselves because they hold them to be ideologically in error. Experience shows that of all kinds of hatred, that based on an ideology is the most rabid. Personal hatred, on the other hand, arises from temporary factors, and seldom takes long to dissipate in the ordinary course of events. But there is little chance of ideological hatred abating. And its target is the obliteration of enemies. Not until this end is achieved will it ever die down. This is the reason that ideological hatred takes no time in assuming the shape of violence. When it is found that peaceful means of persuasion are showing no results, arms are then resorted to, so that all enemies may be removed from its path.

Terrorism in the Name of Islam

At the present time, Muslim fundamentalists are responsible for actions resulting from hatred and marked by violence taking place in the name of Islam. A justification of what they are engaged in is presented in the following couplet by the famous poet Iqbal:

> To every vein of falsehood every Muslim is like a
> surgical knife. (*Shikwa Jawab-e-Shikwah*).

Conversely, however, we find a different picture in the Quran: "When it is said to them: 'Do not commit evil in the land,' they reply: 'We do nothing but good.' But it is they who are the evil-doers, though they may not perceive it." (2:11).

They hold that the aim of Islam is to establish an ideal society and an ideal state. But since, by their lights, this task cannot be performed without political strength, they feel justified in fighting against those who have captured the seats of power.

Violent movements with this aim were launched on a large scale during the second half of the twentieth century. Their targets were either the non-Muslim rulers or the secular Muslim rulers. But despite great losses in terms of life, wealth and resources, these movements failed to produce any positive results. Their having become counter-productive is in itself a proof that their activities were disapproved of by Islam. This is quite expressly stated in the Quran: "God does not love the transgressors." (2:205).

The fact is that the terms 'ideal state' and 'ideal society' have a wonderful resonance, but their use in the name of Islam is sheer exploitation of Islam. Verse 99 of the sixteenth chapter is quite specific about this. It says: "God enjoins justice, kindness and charity... and forbids indecency, wickedness and oppression." Even more specifically the Quran says that God loves the charitable (2:195). And indeed idealism and perfection are highly desirable virtues in Islam, but the direct target of Islamic idealism is not society, and not the state, but the individual.

The perennial objective of the Islamic movement is to strive to make each single individual an ideal human being. Each individual has to be urged to become an example of the 'sublime character' as projected by the Prophet Muhammad, and described in the Quran. (68:4). So far as the ideal society or the ideal state is concerned, it is in no way a direct goal of Islam.

Society and the State are not in themselves independent entities, each being dependent on the mettle of the individuals of which they are constituted. According to a tradition, the Prophet observed: "As you will be, so will be your rulers." (*Mishkat al-Masabih*, 11/1097).

If the establishment of an ideal State were the actual target of Islam, there should, accordingly, be express injunctions to this effect in the Quran and *hadith*. For instance, there should be verses of this type in the Quran: "O Muslims, you are enjoined to establish an ideal State." But there is no such verse and neither is there a single *hadith* which could lead to this conclusion. The references put forward by the upholders of this concept are all inferential in nature, whereas according to Islamic jurisprudence, on the issue of any basic Islamic injunction, inferential argument is in no way valid. Such argument is for peripheral matters and not for basics.

There is another important point in this connection. Those who uphold the establishment of an ideal State to be the goal of Islam ought to learn this lesson from the early period of Islam that this aim was neither achieved in this ideal period nor was it achievable. Those who present the first phase of Islam to be that of an ideal society or an ideal State have fallen prey to a fallacy. They present the example of ideal individuals, equating them with the ideal society or the ideal State. The truth of the matter is that both are totally different from each other.

It is undeniable that in every period of Islamic history, we find large numbers of ideal individuals, and this is true even today. But the ideal State is in no way the goal of Islam and neither has such an State ever existed in the ideal sense of the word. For instance, the first and foremost matter in the setting up of a state is the appointment of the head of a state. But there is no prescribed procedure for such an appointment. The Prophet was succeeded by four rightly guided Caliphs, but every one of them was selected by a different process, for the simple reason that no prescribed method existed at all. This also explains why no tradition could be established for the appointment of the caliphs.

This does not mean, however, that there is something lacking in Islam, or in Islamic principles. The truth is that this very point serves as a proof of Islam being a divine religion, and not of human invention. Islam, according to its own claim, is a religion created by God, which is completely in consonance with nature.(30:30).

The Quran tells us that one proof of its being a book of God is that there is not the slightest inconsistency in its teachings.(4:82). Another proof of this claim is that the target of the Islamic mission set forth by it is the building of ideal individuals and not ideal state.

In fact, man has been created in this world for the special purpose of being put to the test. According to the Quran, the present world is a trial ground and the *Akhirah* (the Hereafter) is the place of reward. As a necessary prerequisite, man has been given total freedom of action.

(33:72). That is to say that he is entirely at liberty either to submit to God or to become a transgressor. (18:29)

According to the creation plan of God, freedom, or free will is every man's birthright, and even if he misuses this power, it will not be taken away from him. It is not part of God's plan of creation ever to abrogate this free will. And it must be conceded that it is this freedom which is the ever-recurring stumbling block in the establishment of an ideal society or an ideal State. For even a handful of men, by misusing their freedom, can disturb the whole of society. That is why the target set by Islam is exactly in accordance with nature, that is, the reform of the individual.

If, on the contrary, the Muslims had been given the mission of establishing an ideal society, or an ideal State, that would have been so unnatural as to be quite impossible. Islam has, therefore, given Muslims a target which is practicable and which, in consequence, does not oblige them to come into conflict with nature. The violence which marks the activities of Muslim fundamentalist groups is the result of not keeping in mind this wisdom of Islam. If you aim at the reform purely of the individual, you will not need to resort to violence for the achievement of your goal. For the task of reforming the individual can be carried on, from beginning to end, in an atmosphere of peaceful persuasion. Whereas the struggle to change the system of the State, being a subversive activity, necessarily leads to war and violence.

Well-known examples of peaceful persuasion were the movements launched by the Sufis, the target of which was not the state, but the individual. Their task involved the spiritual reform of people's hearts and minds, so that they might lead their lives as new, transformed human beings. Thanks to their adherence to this wise policy, the Sufis did not need to resort to violence. Another example in our times is provided by the Tablighi Jamaat, which has been working peaceably on a large scale in the sphere of individual reform.

Since Islamic fundamentalists target the Islamization of the State rather than the reform of individuals, their only plan of action is in the very first instance to launch themselves on a collision course with the rulers who hold sway over the institution of the State. In this way, their movement takes the path of violence from day one. Then all the other evils creep in which are the direct or indirect result of violence, for instance, mutual hatred and disruption of the peace, waste of precious resources, and so on.

It would be right and proper to say that Islam is a name for peaceful struggle, while so-called Islamic fundamentalism is quite the reverse. From the foregoing details it is quite clear that violence, far from arising from the teachings of Islam, is a direct product of Islamic fundamentalism.

Fundamental Principles of Islam

If we are to put 'fundamentalism' in the correct perspective, we should be clear about what actually constitutes the fundamental principles of Islam. There is a *hadith* which gives us clear guidance on this subject. The Prophet observed that Islam is founded on five pillars: Bearing witness that there is no god but the one God and that Muhammad ﷺ is God's Messenger; the regular saying of prayers (*salat*); alms-giving (*zakat*); performing a pilgrimage to the Kabah, the House of God in Makkah (*hajj*) and fasting for the month of Ramadan (*sawm*).

These then are the fundamental principles, or pillars of Islam. The rest of the teachings fall into the category of detailed explanations of and elaborations upon the five basic principles. Holding any other precept besides these to form part of the basic tenets of Islam is misguided and unacceptable.

On further investigation, we find that these five basic teachings have a spirit as well as a form and, what is of real significance is that the true essence of Islam resides not in its outward forms but in its inner spirit. That is why our actions, according to a *hadith*, must be judged by their intentions alone. (*Sahih al-Bukhari*).

Let us take the first of the above principles, which is the article of faith (*kalima*).. The form it takes is the utterance of certain words, expressing one's faith. But this verbal expression is not in itself sufficient. It is essential that at the same time, the concerned person should be imbued with the actual spirit of the words he utters. As we find in the Qur'an: "The Arabs of the desert declare: 'We believe,' 'You do not.' Say rather: 'We profess Islam,' for faith has not yet found its way into your hearts.' (49:4). This shows that to God the real faith (*iman*) is that which reaches into the deepest recesses of the heart; which awakens human consciousness in such a way as to bring to the individual the realization of God. That is to say that the concept of form here is relative, while the concept of spirit is what truly matters.

In the case too of prayer (*salat*), we know that prayer likewise has a fixed form and is to be observed at stipulated

times. But here too it is not the adherence to form in the
repetition of prayer, or the postures adopted, but the spirit
pervading the performance of these rites which is of
overriding importance. That is why the Quran says:
"Successful indeed are the believers who are humble in
their prayers." (23:3). It is essential, therefore, that the ritual
of prayer be imbued with the proper spirit.

The third pillar of Islam, alms-giving (*zakat*), that is to
say, the payment of a fixed amount from one's earnings to
others who are in greater need, is again apparently an act
of pure formality, but according to the Quran, the inner
spirit of *zakat* is fear of God. The Quran describes the
believers as "those who dispense their charity with their
hearts full of fear...." (23:60)

As we know, the pilgrimage to Makkah *(hajj)*, the
fourth pillar of Islam, is organized along particular lines,
according to the rites and rituals of *hajj*. But believers are
made aware at all times that it is not just mere presence in
Makkah and the physical accomplishment of the rites
which really matter, but the circumspect conduct
accompanying each act, the restrained and disciplined
behaviour which reveals the earnest intentions of the
pilgrim to lead a righteous life then and throughout the rest
of the year. Again it is the spirit of the thing which counts.

The fifth pillar of Islam, fasting (*sawm*) for the whole
of the month of Ramadan, is not concerned merely with
abstinence from food and drink during each day from
sunrise to sunset, but with the devotion and gratitude to
God which self-denial teaches (2:183). Thus the essence of
fasting is to produce the spirit of piety. In the words of the
hadith, a fast without this spirit is only the experience of

hunger and thirst. As such, it is not a true fast in the religious sense of the word. *(Mishkat al-Masabih).*

That these are the five fundamentals of Islam has been made quite clear by the Prophet himself. Furthermore, what is desirable in the observance of all of these five pillars is the internal spirit and not the external form. Now if certain people take it upon themselves to revive these five fundamentals of Islam, their endeavours will be confined to an entirely peaceful sphere of activity. At no stage would they ever reach the point of resorting to violence and aggression. The inner spirit which is meant to pervade all actions stemming from the observance of these principles can only be inculcated by advice, counselling and well-reasoned argument. There is no other viable way of achieving this objective save that of peaceful striving.

Islam and Politics

In making an assessment of Islam in relation to politics, one crucial point must be taken into consideration, and that is that politics is only a relative and not the real part of Islam. This difference between a real and a relative feature is that what is essential is relevant in all circumstances and at all times, whereas the relative is required only in relation to particular sets of circumstances. Wherever such circumstances do not exist, relative features lose their relevance and therefore their desirability. This difference between the real and relative is illustrated by the Quranic injunction to perform the Hajj pilgrimage: "Pilgrimage to the House of God is a duty to God for all who can make the journey." (3:97).

The wording of the command to perform Hajj shows

that it is not obligatory for all believers in any absolute sense. It is obligatory rather for those who have the means and the resources, and who are in good enough health to reach the place of pilgrimage. Neither does this injunction even imply that those who do not have the means should make superhuman efforts to find the wherewithal for the journey, so that they may perform this ritual worship. This injunction means that those who have the means should perform the pilgrimage and those who have not will not only be exempted, but will not even be held to account for having failed to do so.

The same is true of politics. That is, if a group of Muslims find themselves in a position to establish the political system of Islam by peaceful methods, and without any violence, then the Shariah will require them to do exactly that. But for those who do not find themselves in such a position, it is not their bounden duty to establish an Islamic political system, nor are they required to set in motion political initiatives calculated to create opportunities to do so.

That is why the Quran at no point gives the following command: "O Muslims, establish the political system of Islam." On the contrary, the Quran makes such clear statements about government and politics as prove that they are relative and not the real parts of Islam. For instance, addressing the believers the Quran says:

> God has promised those of you who believe and do good works that He will make them masters in the land as He had made their ancestors before them, in order to strengthen the faith He chose for them, and to change their state of fear to a sense

of security. Let them worship Me and no other
gods besides Me. Wicked indeed are those who
after this deny Me. (24:55)

From this it is abundantly clear that political power is
a gift from God and is far from being a matter of a goal to
be attained by human efforts. That is, it is not the Islamic
way to launch movements with the aim of achieving
political ascendancy. On the contrary, the objective of the
Islamic struggle is to inculcate in people the Islamic
character and the true spirit of Islam. And then, if, in any
given society, a large number of people were to become
imbued with this true spirit, a time might come when God
in His wisdom saw fit to invest them with political
authority.

Similarly, the Quran says for the benefit of the believers:
"God is powerful and mighty: He will assuredly help those
who, once made masters in the land, will attend to their
prayers and pay the alms tax, enjoin justice and forbid
evil." (22:41).

From the following verse also, we learn from God's
injunction to the Prophet that the matter of political power
rests entirely in the hands of God: "Say, Lord, Sovereign
of all sovereignty, You bestow sovereignty on whom You
will, and take it away from whom You please." (3:26).

That is why political power cannot be the goal to which
believers direct their efforts. The first and foremost duty of
the believers is for all of them, as individuals and without
exception, to fulfill their personal obligations to the utmost
extent. Afterwards, if circumstances are conducive, and
they receive political power purely by the grace of God, the
responsibility of moral governance will fall upon them, as
is mentioned in the above-quoted verse.

It must be conceded that the establishment of an Islamic State is the responsibility not of individuals but of the society to which they belong. In Islam there are certain injunctions of an individual and personal nature, such as ritual fasting, which depend solely upon the will of the individual for their accomplishment. But the establishment of a political system on the basis of Islam depends upon the will of society as a whole. Only if there is a Muslim society possessed of the collective will to accept and institute Islamic government can a political system based on Islam, with all its social caveats, be established.

The Challenge of Fundamentalism

With reference to the Muslims of the present day, the news most highlighted in the media relates to Muslim fundamentalism. Experience has shown that there is nothing more destructive than fanaticism—the driving force of Muslim fundamentalism. However, it is not generally appreciated that Islamic fundamentalism, launched in the name of Islam, has been dealing a death blow to the image of Islam as a religion of peace and mercy. For it is this Muslim fundamentalism which, today, has converted the image of Islam into one tarnished by violence.

Let us place this form of extremism in a historical perspective. At the time of the emergence of modern western civilization, the greater part of the world was politically dominated by Muslims. The Ottoman empire at the western extremity and the Mughal empire on the eastern border had become symbols of glory for the Muslim ummah. These Muslim empires came into direct conflict with the western empires and, in the long run, the

Muslim empires were vanquished. This brought to an end 1000 years of their political supremacy. People in general tend to accept what they see on the surface, so that Muslims all over the world came to hold that, in the break-up of their empires, the upholders of western civilization were the oppressors, while the Muslims were the oppressed.

However, in actual fact, the internal degeneration of these Muslim empires had reduced them to the state of wood infested with white ants. It would only have been a matter of time before they collapsed on their own. It was only by a fortuitous concatenation of events that the military might of western civilization was ostensibly the cause of their fall.

Be that as it may, the upshot of this was that the entire Muslim world became averse to western nations. At an earlier period this aversion had already manifested itself towards the British and the French, and then somewhat later towards the U.S.A., for, in actuality, it is the Americans who have been leading western civilization since the end of the second world war.

Now, I should like to identify and analyse the origin of the present extremist aspect of Islamic fundamentalism, which has made such a rapid descent into violence. The principal reason for its having come into being in this virulent form has its roots in a certain defeatist mentality which has, unfortunately, been developing in the Muslims since the loss of their empires. A defeatist, or a besieged mentality inevitably opts for a negative course of action. The possessors of such a mentality consider themselves as the oppressed, and those whom they see as setting themselves up against them as the oppressors. With this bent of mind, they are willing to engage themselves in any activity whatsoever, no matter how damaging to humanity or contrary to religion it might be.

What made matters worse—as a direct result of this negative psychology—was the emergence of certain Muslim leaders in the first half of the twentieth century, who expounded their own political interpretation of Islam, according to which Islam was a complete system of State and Muslims had been appointed by God to fulfill the mission of establishing this Islamic state throughout the world. Some well-known names associated with this interpretation are the following: Syed Qutub in Egypt, Ayatullah Khomeini in Iran and Syed Abul Ala Maududi in Pakistan.

This political view of Islam, in spite of being a grave misinterpretation, spread rapidly among Muslims. The only reason for this was that Muslims, owing to their defeatist mentality, saw nothing incongruous in its negativity. Given the circumstances of their past history, this political interpretation was in total consonance with their psychological condition. Thus, due to their negative mindset—and not to Islamic reasoning—this false interpretation soon gained currency among them, and the activities which were an offshoot from this—paradoxical as this may seem—were backed by funding from America in a bid to stem the rising tide of communism.

Prior to 1991, when the Soviet Union had assumed the position of a super power, and posed a continuing threat to America, one of the strategies adopted by America was to play off the Muslim fundamentalists against the communists, because these fundamentalists were persistently writing and speaking against communism as being the enemy of Islam. America also gave all kinds of help, to the fundamentalists. It provided them with weapons to set themselves up against the Soviet Union and assisted in the dissemination of their literature all over the world. But this enemy-of-my-enemy-is-a-friend formula ultimately proved counter-productive, in that it virtually amounted to replacing one enemy with another. The waging of this proxy war turned out to be only very temporary in its benefits.

Those who at a later stage felt the impact of extremist fundamentalism, took this to be a case of violence against them. So they opted for a policy of gun versus gun. But subsequent events proved this policy to be a total failure, the reason being that the issue was not that of conducting a purely physical struggle, but of exposing and scotching the fallacies of a flawed ideology. You can win a fight with arms, but to defeat an ideology, a counter-ideology is a *sine qua non*. Without that nothing can be achieved.

There is no doubt about it that Muslim fundamentalism is a threat to peace, for, due to their fanaticism, its proponents do not stop sort of resorting to destructive activity, even if it should prove suicidal. Now the task we must undertake is to make use of the media on all fronts in order to make people aware of the fact that this political interpretation of Islam is totally without basis either in the Quran or in the examples set by the Prophet in thought, word and deed. As opposed to this erroneous interpretation, the true values of Islam, based on peace, brotherhood and well-wishing should be presented to the public. If this correct interpretation of Islam could be brought to people's attention, I should have high hopes that the majority of the people who have been misguided would abandon the path of hatred and violence and come back to Islam—"to the home of peace" to which God calls us in the Quran.

It is true that in these violent activities only a small group is involved. But this small group has the indirect support of the majority, who are no less swayed by the political interpretation of Islam. According to Khalil Gibran, "not a single leaf falls from the tree without the silent consent of the whole tree." If then the majority were to withdraw its indirect support and condemn Islamic militancy, these fringe groups would lose their moral courage. That would be the first step. Then the time would come when the fundamentalists who are directly involved in violent activities would abandon the path of violence altogether.

13

❦

The Shariah and Its Application

After going through some articles on *da'wah* by this author on the internet, one reader sent his strong reaction by e-mail. He rejected the point of view expressed in a hard-hitting manner. By citing certain instances from the article, he wrote that the point of view advocated by the author was quite contradictory to the Quran. The following is a part of that he had to say :

> Maulana Wahiduddin says: Muslims should exercise patience against atrocities committed by other nations and engage themselves in *da'wah* work. Whereas in the Quran, in sharp contrast to this point of view, God Almighty says:
>
> And fight them until there is no more *fitnah*, and religion becomes Allah's, in its entirety (8:39)
>
> Then, whom we are to pay heed to, Allah or Maulana Wahiduddin?

This appears to be quite damning. But in reality, it is a total misapprehension.The error can be made plain if we may suppose for a while that if a complete Quran had been in people's possession in Makkah, as it is in the possession of the person mentioned above, there might have arisen the same confusion in Makkah.

We find from traditions that in the early phase of Islam in Makkah, when the Makkan pagans had begun their cruel persecution of the Muslims, certain of the faithful, reacting to this grievous injustice, asked the Prophet's permission to do battle with their persecutors. But the Prophet went on exhoring them to exercise patience, saying: "I have been commanded only to perform *da'wah*, communication of the message of God. I have not been given permission to do battle." If the complete Quran in bound form had existed at that time, someone might have stood up and said: "See, Muhammad ﷺ is asking us to exercise patience, while in the Quran God asks us to do battle with our opponents." But no such thing took place in Makkah, for the simple reason that people did not possess the complete Quran as they do today.

This example shows wherein, those who raise such objections, have gone wrong. The actual error lies in their taking something out of context by misquoting the verses of the Quran. At a time when Muslims are in the stage of *da'wah* and as such are might have required to perform their *da'wah* responsibilities by exercising patience, they have been mistakingly referring to the verses revealed to discharge the responsibilities at the stage of defence. In this way they have fallen into the error of wrong application of the verses. They are citing the verses applicable to such circumstances as prevailed in Madinah, while they find themselves in the situation that prevailed in Makkah.

History shows that the Prophet of Islam and his companions were faced with all the problems and hardships in Makkah, as the Muslims of modern times have allegedly been, facing. Yet when the Prophet of Islam asked his companions to follow the path of patience and avoidance, no one stood up to question why they must exercise patience, when the Quran enjoins them to do battle, simply because the complete Quran was not available. The truth is that the Quran was not revealed all at once in the form of a bound book, the one we have in our possession today. The Quran was revealed on different occasions over a period of 23 years, but in instalments.   Only those commands were revealed to the Prophet as were required by the circumstances. For instance, in the initial stage, the Prophet was given the command to perform *da'wah* by observing patience (74:2-7) .Later on, as circumstances warranted, the command to migrate was revealed. (16:41). Subsequently when circumstances further, changed the command to do battle was revealed (2:190), etc.

This shows that in the initial stage of Islam when the Quran was being revealed, the order of revelation tallied with the order of events. For this reason people did not find any difficulty in understanding their role as soon as a command was revealed. But afterwards, all the verses revealed over a period of 23 years, relating to different sets of circumstances, were collected together in the form of a bound volume. It is this complete book which has remained in the hands of later Muslim generations till today.

By the very law of nature circumstances keep changing,

and this fact must be borne in mind that the divine book
we possess comprised of revelations made at different
times and collected together in the form of the Quran. These
scriptures contain various commands, injunctions
pertaining to all kinds of situations — all collected together
in one book. Then how are Muslims of later times supposed
to receive guidance from the Quran?

The answer is that the study of Quranic verses should
be done in the light of the causes of revelation (*asbabal-
nuzul*). That is, first of all, those in search of guidance
should determine objectively the state of affairs in a given
situation, then strive to find the verse or verses revealed
in a similar situation in the first phase of Islam. And when
that injunction is found, it should be applied to the present
situation. That is, the purpose served by the immediate
revelation in the first phase, will now be served by pin-
pointing *similarity* between the past and the present
situations.

For a better understanding of this, one should take into
account the four different stages of the period of
prophethood of the Prophet of Islam :

(a) The first half of the Makkan period;
(b) The second half of the Makkan period;
(c) The first half of the Madinan period;
(d) The second half of the Madinan period.

Basically these four periods keep repeating themselves
throughout human history. By studying the Quran in
depth, the parallels to present-day circumstances can
easily be discovered: it is very necessary if guidance is to
be received from the Quran in later periods of history.

As mentioned above, the Quran which exists with us

today in its complete form was not available to the Muslims during the lifetime of the Prophet. Instead it was revealed in parts (instalments). At that time only those passages of the Quran were revealed which were relevant to the circumstances, that is, whatever command was required pertaining to the actual situation only that was given to the believers. This way the believers had no problem in understanding their tasks and subsequently devoted themselves to performing them without any questioning.

For instance, when circumstances required full attention to be paid to the task of *da'wah*, this verse was revealed:

Lead all men to the path of your Lord with wisdom and mild exhortation. (16:25).

Therefore all the followers of the Prophet adopted *da'wah* as a single point formula and became engaged in this task with complete dedication. Similarly, when the circumstances required patience and fortitude, this verse was revealed:

Bear up then with patience, as did the steadfast Apostles before you. (46:35).

Subsequently, the believers adopted an attitude of patience with total devotion and concentration. Similarly when, in the wake of aggression by the other party, the problem of defence arose, this verse was revealed in the Quran:

Fight for the sake of God those that fight against you (2:190).

On receiving this command, all the believers engaged themselves wholeheartedly in the field of battle.

This same pattern continued throughout the prophetic

period lasting 23 years. Each time only that part of the Quran was revealed which was required in regard to the circumstances. The believers of this first phase were solely concerned with carrying out the particular commandment relevant to given situation.

They were not required to decide as to which of the various and different commandments were applicable. But, in later times, the state of affairs changed. Now, all the parts of the Quran revealed on different occasions were collected and bound in the form of one book. That is to say, the commands and their background had been separated from one another. Afterwards the responsibility devolved upon the Muslims themselves, by means of deep reflection and study, to strive to ascertain which of the injunctions was applicable to them in particular situations. Thus by discovering the relevant verse of the Quran, they should follow with unstinting devotion and dedication. Believers are urged "to listen to the Quran with attention, holding their peace." (7:204).

That is, they must pay full heed to the passage of the Quran revealed to the Prophet and then wholeheartedly carry out the command. The latter day Muslims have been charged with the added responsibility of inference (see the Quran, 4:83) and *ijtihad* (striving) as mentioned in the *Hadith*. That is, to reflect with the utmost honesty, sincerity and God-fearingness as to pinpoint which divine command is addressed to them in relation to the state of affairs in which they find themselves at that point in time, and then to strive to carry out that command without showing any reluctance.

That is to say, in the first phase of Islam, the injunction

of *da'wah* was revealed at the time when the performance of *da'wah* was required, the injunction of patience was revealed when patience was required and the injunction to do battle was revealed at the time when battle was required. Thus people were not faced with any confusion in understanding the injunctions as well as their application. But latter-day Muslims find out the injunctions—of patience, *da'wah* and war—all together in one single book. It was now left to Muslims to find, on their own, which of the varied injunctions is relevant to their particular sets of circumstances. That is to say, earlier the circumstances and the injunctions tallied with one another, whereas now the injunctions are many and varied, while the state of affairs in any one particular given situation demands, (in practice), the application of only one injunction.

As mentioned above, the present Quran does not follow the order of revelation, that is, the chronological order of revelations has not been followed in the compilation of the Quran.

The arrangement of the present order of the Quran not being based on the order of revelation is probably a matter of testing the faithful. This test requires Muslims to exercise their reason objectively in order to find out which one of the commands it is desirable for them to carry out in a particular situation. This test in its nature is like that given to the people of the first phase. In their case it involved the discovery of the true claimant to Truth out of many claimants. Similarly, the test of the Muslims of later times involved the discovery of that particular injunction applicable to their circumstances and desirable by God. The emergence of the Prophet was a test for his contemporaries to see if they could recognise the true guide, while the arrangement of the Quran based on a non-revelationary order serves to test people, on whether they can discover true guidance or not. Latter-day Muslims have to pass this test in exactly the same way as the people of the first phase passed a test of the same nature.

The Prophet and the believers of his time lived in Makkah in the early stage of his prophethood. At that time the idolatrous leaders of Makkah enjoyed the dominant position. They used to persecute the Prophet and the other Muslims. Now the question was as to what the believers should resort to in those circumstances. In that situation they were guided by God to say: "We will endure your persecution patiently. In Allah, let all the faithful put their trust." (14:12).

That is, they had to adhere to the way of patience and forbearance regardless of the injustice and oppression of their opponents.

In this way, by timely guidance, the believers learnt what their policy should be in whatever circumstances they found themselves in. They understood fully that even if the other party was guilty of injustice, they had unilaterally to maintain an attitude of patience.

Then the time came when the Prophet and his companions migrated to Madinah, leaving their hometown. The circumstances changed. The injunctions too changed according to the new circumstances. Earlier the guidance given was to exercise patience on being persecuted, now the guidance to deal with persecution changed. The command given in the Quran on this occasion was: "Permission (to take up arms) is hereby given to those who are attacked." (22:39).

This shows that at times defence is required to deal with persecution. Whereas at other times no counter move is desirable except for patience. Now the question arises as to how to find out in which circumstance the way of patience and tolerance has to be adopted and in which circumstance doing battle in self-defence is to be resorted to.

The believers of the first phase did not need to take any decision regarding the answer to these questions. For the answers according to the prevailing state of affairs continued to be revealed by God. But this situation no longer prevailed for latter-day Muslims. For them the questions exist in relation to the circumstances, but the answers have to be found by their own questing.

Herein lies the test of the believers of later times. If the test of the people of the Prophet's day consisted of recognising the Prophet, the test of the latter-day Muslims lies in recognising the command of the Prophet. The Quran enshrines verses on both kinds of injunctions together in the same volume. Now it is the responsibility of the believers themselves to reflect deeply, objectively, without any bias, to find which of the commands is to be applied to any given situation and which of the commands is to be considered abrogated for the time being. This nature of the command was earlier determined directly by revelation, while now this has to be determined by the exercise of ijtihad.

Let's take up another aspect of this subject. The idolaters were there in Makkah when the Prophet and his companions lived in the city, and it was the same idolaters who lived in Makkah after the migration of the Prophet up until the conquest of Madinah.

But the policy for dealing with them changed in the second of these two phases. History shows that the command given in regard to these idolaters in the first phase was simply to warn them by adopting peaceful means: "Arise and warn, call them to the path of their Lord with wisdom." According to this injunction, the Prophet and his companions used to visit those people in Makkah and recite to them the verses of da'wah from the Quran. They used to address their gatherings in these words: "Say there is no God but God and you will earn salvation."

But after the migration and the conquest of Makkah, the situation changed. Now chapter nine of the Quran, titled 'Repentance', was revealed which conveyed a "declaration of immunity by Allah and His Messenger to the idolaters with whom you have made agreements."

After the revelation of this chapter, when the time of Hajj (pilgrimage) came the Prophet sent a delegation of his companions to Makkah to make a public pronouncement of this declaration from God.

From this example we find that when the da'wah or the communication of the message was required in regard to the idolaters, the verses dealing with da'wah were revealed. In this way, the knowledge of the very order of revelation sufficed to indicate what had to be done and when.

But the position of latter-day Muslims is different. Now the state of affairs is that the entire Quran is in our hands in the form of one collected volume, containing both kinds of verses together. Muslims have,therefore, to discover from their own ijtihad which of the injunctions are addressed to them in the particular set of circumstances in which they find themselves.

This is the test of the latter-day Muslims. Their success lies in their ability to discover that particular injunction which is desirable by God in terms of their circumstances. Their failure lies in their inability to discover this injunction desirable in their changed sets of circumstances. For instance, in terms of their actual state of affairs, the verses of patience and *da'wah* are applicable to them, yet they are waging war with other nations by referring to the verses on fighting in the Quran. Such an act on their part amounts to their having failed in the divine test.

This failure is very grave in nature. This can be likened to a Prophet's contemporary failing to recognise him as the true Prophet of God. The deprivation resulting from this failure is very serious while the gains resulting from success in recognizing is very great.

The Secret of Guidance and Ignorance

The Quran states, "By it* God causes many to stray and many He leads into the Right Path." (2:26).

The Quran is, without doubt, a Truth from God. Then why is it that some find guidance from it, while others are lead astray? The chief reason for this difference lies in the difference in reference. If the Quran is studied with reference to the correct context, the reader will receive guidance. On the contrary, if the reference is changed, the same Quran will become the cause of people's going astray.

Studying the different parts of Quran in the correct perspective is to study them in the light of the traditions

---

* The Quran

of the causes of revelation i.e. to understand the background of the verses. A number of traditions have been recorded in the books of *Hadith* and Tafsir which tell us which verse or verses of the Quran were revealed on which particular occasions. These traditions providing the background are not only conducive to understanding the initial message, but also serve as a reliable guide as regards their correct application in later times in similar situations.

Studying the Quran with reference to the traditions of the causes of revelation does not imply that the Quran was a book of an ephemeral nature. What is meant is that the initial nature of a command should be properly understood in order to discover its vaster application, so that it may be correctly applied at a later date.

Most of the injunctions in the Quran are brief in nature. For instance, the Quran states:

> Believers, if an evil-doer brings you a piece of news, inquire first into its truth, lest you should wrong others unwittingly and repent of what you have done (49:6).

According to the traditions of the causes of revelation this verse was revealed following a particular incident. But the verse neither mentions that incident nor the people involved in it. In order, therefore, to understand the actual meaning and message of the verse, it is essential to study it in the light of that particular incident—the cause of the revelation.

In this way, that incident mentioned in detail in traditions gives us the knowledge of the background in the light of which we can properly understand the real nature of the injunction revealed in the concerned verses. When the original context of an injunction is properly understood, the application of the same to similar incidents taking place in later times is greatly facilitated. We are then able to understand what the Quranic injunction would be in a situation which is similar to the one referred to in the Quran.

The verse of the Quran mentioned earlier tells us that just as the Quran is a source of guidance to people, so also does it become a source of leading them astray. Who are these people who are lead astray. These are the people who do not study the Quran in its proper context. Studying of the Quran in this way means to study it in the light of one's own whims and desires, instead of in the light of the causes of revelation.

If we study the verses of the Quran in reference to the causes of revelation, the reality dawns upon us that the target of Islam is not to exterminate the opponents of Islam, but rather to help them enter the fold of Islam by our performing *da'wah*. This verse of the Quran gives us a clear guideline in this regard:

"And who is better in speech than one who calls men to Allah, works righteously, and says, 'I am of those who surrender to Him.' Good and evil deeds are not alike. Requite evil with good, and he, between whom and you is enmity, will become your dearest friend. But none will attain this save those who endure with fortitude and are of the greatest good fortune. And if a malicious attempt is made by the devil to tempt you, seek refuge in Allah. He hears all and knows all." (41:33-36).

Understanding the background to the revelations is, therefore, extremely important in order to receive guidance from the Quran. If the verses of the Quran are studied without the help of those traditions, each verse will appear to be giving an absolute command (an injunction in the absolute sense). But when we study the Quran in the light of those traditions which give us the background of revelations, we come to know that they had specific application. Whenever any difficult situation arose, during the life time of the Prophet, a revelation would come in relation to it.

In such a state of affairs it is not proper to take any given verse of the Quran in an absolute sense and apply it to latter-day situations. It is therefore essential to study the verses of the Quran in the light of the causes of revelation. After learning the background we can apply them to any similar situation produced in later times. According to this principle, taking the verses of the Quran in their proper context is a source of guidance, while doing the reverse is a source of transgression.

In short, the Quran is a compendium of various and varied kinds of injunctions. For instance, at one place we find this injunction in the Quran: "Avoid the polytheists" (15:94). At another place we will find this injunction: "Fight against the idolaters as they fight against you." (9:16)

Both these injunctions are apparently contradictory to one another. So the question arises as to which command should be followed by a reader of today.

The background to the revelation provides the answer. All the injunctions in the Quran have been revealed on specific occasions. The traditions dealing with the background of the verses tell us which injunction was revealed on which occasion. In this way, by a study of the background of the verses, we can discover the first application of the Quranic injunctions. And when the first application is properly understood, having an exact knowledge of the second application is greatly facilitated. A proper understanding of the first application paves the way for total correctness in the second application.

Now what we have to do is, whenever we find ourselves in any set of circumstances calling for Quranic solutions, we must make a thorough study of the traditions dealing with the background of the verses. This will enable us to discover which of the verses were revealed in the Quran (that is, which injunction was given to them on that occasion) when the companions of the Prophet were faced with the same set of circumstances. In this way it is the element of *similarity* between the two situations which guides us as to which verse or verses are addressed to us in the circumstances we are faced with. That is, in the light of first application we must determine the second application.

14

❧❦❧

Spirituality in Islam

What is spirituality? — or *rabbaniyat*, to use the Qur'anic term. It is the elevation of the human condition to a plane on which the mind is focused on the higher, non-material realities of a godly existence. The opposite of spirituality is materialism, a course followed all too often in this world. One who takes this course, giving all his attention to worldly things, or to put it another way, who centres his attention on mere appearances, is regarded as being materially-minded. Conversely, one who rises above material things or appearances, who finds his focus of interest in non-material things, is regarded as being spiritual or godly. The latter is one who obeys the injunction of the Qur'an: "Be devoted servants of God" (3:79) or, alternatively, "O people, be godly servants of Allah."

To understand what constitutes materialism, imagine that you come across a palatial house, or see an attractive car being driven along the street. If a strong desire is kindled within you to have such things in your possession, that is clear indication that materialism is a major motivating factor in your life. One who sees the same things, but remains unaffected by the notions of luxury that they convey, and therefore feels no desire to acquire them, lives in a more rarefied sphere in which materialism plays no part. He sees no attraction in the lesser world of material appearances, being engrossed in the higher realities of the supremely spiritual life. The truly non-material person is never influenced by superficialities: his soul exists at too profound a level of spirituality.

This is true, and without any exaggeration. Those who live for worldly pleasures believe that gratification cannot be had except from material things. But this thinking is due to sheer ignorance. Worldly pleasure being the only thing they have experienced, they imagine that for enjoyment they must depend solely on material things. Had they experienced spiritual pleasure, they would certainly have forgotten material pleasure. The pleasure to be derived from material things is limited in nature and very short-lived. Whereas spiritual pleasure may be eternally savoured.

Eating tasty food certainly gives us a sense of enjoyment. But it is only when the experience of eating such food results in an outpouring of thanksgiving to God that our pleasure knows no bounds. Travelling in a modern car is also enjoyable, but the pleasure which comes from a deep perception of reality,—i.e. the apprehension of the indescribably unique power of God as manifested in the world in the form of cars, aeroplanes and all the other modern amenities created for man's comfort—is far superior to that which one experiences while travelling in a luxurious automobile.

The materially-minded person can find pleasure only in something which he or she actually experiences. But the spiritual person lives on a higher plane. For him, even seeing things in another's possession occasions an outpouring from the innermost recesses of his heart of his gratefulness to God. Another's material pleasure transforms itself into a spiritual pleasure for him as well. A materially-minded person sees only the creature, while a spiritually-inclined person sees the splendour of the Creator through the creature. And it is obvious that the spiritual riches accruing from the discovery of the Creator cannot be gained in the discovery of mere objects of creation.

Furthermore, in the spiritual world there is no great difference between comfort and deprivation. What one gains from experiences of material pleasure is of far less value than what one gains from experiences of deprivation. The tears of pain flowing from an aching heart gives far greater satisfaction than the laughter of happiness. The greatest source of pleasure is in the remembrance of God. It is this reality which finds expression in the following verse of the Qur'an: "It is only in the remembrance of God that hearts are comforted." (13:28)

Here comfort means not just the temporary solace to be found in everyday convenience, but the real comfort with its implications of peace of mind that can stem only from God Almighty. Man by nature is an idealistic creature. Anything short of ideal can attract only fitful attention from him, whereas true and lasting comfort can be achieved only through the Perfect Being.

Existing at the level of materialism is like descending into animality. Materialism is, in other words, a form of shallowness. The real man is one who discovers the secret of living on the elevated plane of spirituality. If in materialism there is the pleasure of laughter, in spirituality there is the pleasure of pain. If materialism is to live a life of limitations, spirituality is to live in limitlessness.

The Universe a Source of Divine Inspiration

The universe has been fashioned by God in a way that it may become a source of spiritual inspiration for man. According to the Qur'an it is the quality of tawassum (15:75) that enables one to find inspiration in the universe. What is *tawassum*? It is the ability to understand the signs of nature. That is, to observe the phenomena of the universe in order to draw lessons from them and receive spiritual nourishment from physical events.

Tawassum is, in a sense, a matter of conversion, on a parallel with grass entering the body of the cow and through a natural process being transformed into milk. Similarly, the truly religious person is like a divine industry. He is able to convert physical events into spiritual lessons. He extracts spiritual nourishment from material things.

The distinguishing feature of the wise people described in the Qur'an is that they continuously derive such sustenance from their environment, thus maintaining their intellectual and spiritual well-being. This is elaborated upon in the Qur'an as follows:

"In the creation of the heavens and the earth, and in the succession of night and day, there are signs for men of understanding; those that remember God when standing, sitting, and lying down, and reflect on the creation of the heavens and the earth (saying): 'Lord, You have not created these in vain. Glory be to You! Save us from the torment of the fire, Lord." (3:191)

A Personal Experience

It was Thursday morning, 17th June 1999. I was in Manchester, England, staying in the house of an Arab Brother Alaref Ahmad. While I was sitting in my room on the upper floor, I heard a gentle knock on the door. When I opened it, I found a child of about five years of age. It was Qanita, the first-born daughter of Brother Alaref. She asked, all innocence and gentleness, "Do you need anything?" (turidu haja). Perhaps it was her mother who had sent her, and although this was a simple question, I was quite overwhelmed by this innocent voice; to the extent that I could not utter a single word in reply. This was a normal incident, but in my mind, it became transformed into a supra-normal event. Children are like the flowers of God and little angels. I felt as if God Himself had sent me an angel to discover and meet my needs.

At this moment, a famous hadith came to mind: "Your Lord descends to this worldly haven every day, looks at His servants and says, 'Is there anyone who has a need and asks Me, that I may give it to him?'" (Muslim).

'Do you need anything?' was a short question that came from an innocent soul, but it was enough to cause a great revolution in my inner being; referred to by modern scholars as 'brainstorming.'

For a while, I felt that I could see the whole of the Universe on the screen of my mind. This was a great spiritual experience which could not be expressed in human words. In the beginning, it seemed as though God, through a little angel, was saying, "O my servant, do you need anything?" Then, the matter extended to include the whole Universe with its Heavens and its Earth.

In fact, it was only a little girl at the door of my room, asking, "Do you need anything?" but in its extended sense, it was as if the whole Universe was asking the same question.

The vast Heaven was saying, "Do you need a shelter? Here I am to provide you with one, because God has ordered me to do so." The gleaming sun was saying, "Do you need light? I am here to supply it and transform your darkness into light." The majestic mountains were announcing, "Would you like to be on the highest level in all humanity? I am here at your service to help you attain that high position." The flowing water in the river-beds was murmuring, "Do you want to have a spiritual bath to purify your soul? I am here to offer you that." And the gusting wind was asking, "Do you want to tour the Universe to see the wondrous signs of God? Here is my back for you to ride on to embark on such a Divine journey." The trees were whispering, "Would you like to have a personality as radiant as ours? We are here to make your wish a reality." The fruits on their branches and the crops in their husks were declaring, "If you crave nourishment for your intellectual and spiritual life, we are here to provide you with it."

While this reel was playing in my mind, I heard birds chirping, "O servant of God! Here is good news for you: If you have a need, then God has made the whole Universe to serve your needs. God is so generous that He has created the whole of the Universe to be at your service, day and night. In addition to this, if you show thankfulness to God, He will give you what is greater than all of this — Eternal Paradise in which there will be "...neither fear nor grievance" (6:48).

Then, the following Qur'anic verse came to mind: "And He gave you all that you asked for" (14.34). This means that whatever is needed for Man to live a good life on this Earth has been prepared in advance by God, directly and indirectly. Horses, for instance, were directly created; whereas aeroplanes were provided indirectly. The travelling of the voice through the air is an example of direct provision, while its transmission by means of electronic equipment is a form of indirect provision. Perhaps, this is what is meant by the following Qur'anic verse: "And (He has created) horses, mules and donkeys for you to ride, and as an adornment. And He has created (other) things which are beyond your knowledge" (16:8).

God Almighty says, "O you who believe! Eat of the good things that We have provided for you. And be grateful to Allah, if it is Him you worship" (2:172). This means that God Almighty has created everything, imaginable and unimaginable; great and small, in the most perfect form. Then, He gave all this free to Man. The only price to be paid for these endless blessings is thankfulness; it is Man's recognition, from the depths of his heart, that God is the Giver and Man the receiver.

The Qur'an mentions as examples of God's beneficiaries the people of Saba.' God Almighty gave them a sign in the, "two Gardens to the right hand and to the left; (and it was said to them:) 'Eat of the provision of your Lord, and be grateful to Him: fair is your land and Oft-Forgiving is your Lord'"(34:15). This means that if Man pays the price — that is, gratitude—then not only will he be allowed to avail of these blessings, but more importantly, he will also be rewarded with eternal Paradise, which is a perfect version of this present imperfect world of God.

God Almighty bestowed upon Man all these material things which man needs if he is to live a good life on this Earth. All these things are silently conveying the following message: "O Man! Are you seeking something greater than all this? Do you want spiritual peace in addition to material peace? Do you want a world of perfection after this imperfect world? Would you like to taste the blessings of God in the world of eternity after you have tasted them in this ephemeral world? Do you wish to have all these comforts as a blessing in the world to come, after you have had them as a trial in this transient world? Would you like to realize your full potential after experiencing the limitation of your capacities in this present world?"

God created a perfect and complete world as an eternal abode for Man. Then, He wanted to know who was worthy of inhabiting that eternal world. For this purpose, He created the time-bound and imperfect abode in which we are now living. This life, therefore, is only a test. Man is constantly under the observation of his Lord. With every utterance and movement, Man is writing his own eternal destiny. One who, during his pre-death period proves himself through his conduct deserving of that world will, in his post-death-period, be rewarded with admission into it. Others, however, will be flung into the Universal junkyard, that is Hell, condemned for all eternity. So, they will lose both worlds, the present incomplete world as well as the next, perfect and everlasting world.

God has revealed Himself in two books — the Qur'an and the Universe. The Qur'an is a literal version of God's word, while the Universe, or nature, is a practical demonstration of it. These two are the basic sources of spiritual inspiration for a man who seeks to live a life according to the divine scheme.

This dual source of divine inspiration is mentioned in the Qur'an in the following verse: "God is He who raised the Heavens without visible supports, then He ascended the Throne. He has compelled the sun and the moon to be of service, each pursuing an appointed course; He controls the affairs (of the Universe); He makes plain His revelations, so that you may be certain of the meeting with your Lord." (13:2). So, the Qur'an is like a guidebook. It prepares the mind so that one may properly understand the Universe and live in it as desired by God.

So, a *mu'min* (true believer) has precisely that kind of prepared mind. When he sees the Universe with its various parts functioning in an absolutely coherent manner, he will spontaneously say: "There is no god but the one God!" and when he examines it, he will find that there are so many complex happenings in its vastness. Nevertheless, he finds that every part of the universe is highly predictable. With this discovery, he realizes that it is as if God was suggesting that he himself should have a predictable character. When he observes that the various parts of the Universe function with absolute harmony, he realises that, in like manner, he should live in complete harmony with society; without hatred for or malice towards anyone. When he sees the events of the universe always proceeding towards a meaningful result, he realises that man's life, too, must have a meaningful end. Thus he exclaims: "O our Lord! You have not created (all) this without purpose. Glory be to You! Give us salvation from the torment of Hellfire!" (3:191).

In brief, the universe is a manifestation of the Attributes of Almighty God. Hence, it is a source of spiritual nourishment for those who want to lead a divine life on earth. For them, the whole universe becomes a great means of their reaching spiritual perfection. This spiritual development continues incessantly throughout their earthly life. As the ultimate result of this life-long developmental process, they attain that degree of spirituality which the Qur'an calls the 'Rabbani soul.' It is such as these who, in the life Hereafter, will be told by their most compassionate Lord: "Dwell in Paradise; you shall have no fear, nor shall you grieve." (7:49)

There is nothing mysterious about spirituality in Islam. It is rather the direct result of the kind of intellectual development that takes place when a believer ponders over the Creator and His creation: he gains something in the process that may be termed spirituality. The source, therefore, of Islamic spirituality is perusal and reflection rather than any sort of mysterious exercise.

That is why the Qur'an rejects asceticism (monasticism), referring to it as a bida'a (innovation) in religion which God did not prescribe for people. (57:27)

From the Qur'an we learn that, in the very creation of the universe, the signs of God lie hidden all around us. A person who is in a state of keen awareness when he reflects upon the things of the world comes to see the Creator in the creatures. The meaning of the creation of the Universe is laid bare before him. Ultimately, the universe becomes a permanent source of spiritual inspiration. He is continuously nourished by it during his worldly experience, and his observation of the universe awakens in him latent divine qualities.

The result of this observation and contemplation of the universe does not result in his shunning normal life. Far from withdrawing from the world, he lives in it, participating in all its activities; yet despite his involvement, he remains aloof. That is to say, although he fulfills all his duties and responsibilities, his heart is not attached to worldly affairs. He appears to live in the world, but he stands apart from it. Thanks to this state of his heart, he acquires tremendous spiritual gains. The Prophet Muhammad ﷺ says of such individuals:

> "God plants wisdom in the heart of one who shows disinclination for the world."

There is life for man in spirituality: this is indeed the real life for man.

15

꧁❀꧂

Preservation, Updating, Da'wah

Addressing the Prophet Muhammad ﷺ God Almighty has declared: We have sent you forth as a mercy to all mankind. (21:107). Similarly, the Qur'an states:

> Blessed be He who has revealed *Al-Furqan* (the criterion), that is, the Qur'an, to His servant, so that he may be a warner to all mankind. (25:1)

In another chapter the Qur'an says: "We have sent you forth to all mankind, so that you may give them good news and warn them." (34:28)

These passages in the Qur'an tell us that the Prophet Muhammad ﷺ was sent for all humanity and for all present and future generations. He was appointed by God Almighty to give a divine lead to all mankind, and this process has to be continued, generation after generation, till the last day of the world. During his lifetime he fulfilled this duty directly and, after his death, this task has to be continued indirectly through his Ummah. The task to be performed by later generations has been divided, basically, into three categories:

(a)   Process of Preservation,

(b)   Process of Updating,

(c)   Process of *da'wah*

The goal of the first process is to keep the book brought by the Prophet intact in its original form, generation after generation. There must be no human interpolations and none of its parts should be destroyed.

The first major step in the process of preservation was undertaken, after the passing away of the Prophet, during the life of the first Caliph, Abu Bakr Siddiq. At that time tens of thousands of the companions of the Prophet had learnt the complete Qur'an by heart. It was thus completely preserved in human memory.

But as far as the writing of the Qur'an was concerned, it existed only in fragments on different kinds of writing materials. The first Caliphs, therefore, engaged scholars of the Qur'an from amongst the companions to prepare a single volume of the Qur'an. By employing the double checking system, that is, the Qur'an as memorized was checked with the Qur'an in its written form and the Qur'an in written form was checked with the Qur'an preserved in human memory. Thus the first caliph prepared the first bound volume of the Qur'an, which served as the standard copy. All the later copies of the Qur'an were made from this original volume.

Thus, the Qur'an was preserved by following the double method—writing and memorizing, generation after generation, until it reached the age of the printing press, whereupon any possibility of human interpolation in the text was ruled out.

Contribution of Muhaddithin (Scholars of Hadith)

In addition to this, a huge number of eminent Muslim scholars arose among the first few generations of Islam to prepare a totally authentic and unparalleled historical record generally known as *Hadith*, *Sirah* and *Maghazi*. Within a surprisingly short period of time, they produced a vast and systematic body of literature that contains almost each word uttered by the Prophet, every action done by him, anything approved of or disapproved of by him, including other chronological details about his companions and the succeeding generations. This literature, as a whole, is rightly considered to be the second basic source of Islam after the Qur'an. The authentic part of *Hadith* literature coupled with the Qur'an, provides an all-inclusive text of Islamic ideology. Thus, by both the sources having been committed to writing, the original version of Islam has been so perfectly and permanently preserved, that until the coming of doomsday, anybody can at any time confirm how Islamic teachings were revealed from God, and then how they were explained and practised by the Prophet and his companions.

Religious Institutions

Right from the days of the companions of the Prophet up till the present times the majority of Muslims, both rulers and ruled, have shown the greatest of interest in and concern about imparting a theoretical as well as a practical knowledge of Islam to their offspring. For the purpose of learning how to practise Islam in day-to-day life in accordance with the prophetic role model, numerous institutions came into existence. The religious schools of the traditional type was called a Madrasa, while the spiritual training centre was called a Takya. Starting in the remote past and continuing right up to the present day, a tremendous network of such religious institutions has proliferated all over the Muslim world, and in recent times has been marked with renewed vigour and vitality. Without doubt these institutions have been successful in at least one of their fundamental objectives, that is, to preserve and transmit the practical form or applied aspect of Islam from generation to generation. In the present century, the same purpose has also been achieved by a number of other religious organizations and movements. The movement of Tabligh may be cited here as an example.

Updating

The second point in this connection is the process of updating. The religion handed down by the Prophet remains one and the same. However, since the situations in human society are subject to change, it becomes essential that the original religion (al-din) could be reapplied to changing sets of circumstances. For instance, the shariah permitted the touching of leather socks with wet hands for purification instead of the normal washing of feet during ablution. Now when socks made of artificial fibres came to be used, the question arose as to whether doing masah (rubbing with water) was lawful or not. Then it became necessary to re-apply the old injunction to the new situation; after the exercise of ijtihad, permission was given to do masah on these socks.

In every age the necessity arises of re-applying divine injunctions. And this has happened in modern times on a large scale. In ancient times war was a means of settling conflicts, but with the invention of the latest deadly weapons, war today serves no positive purpose. Now power lies in peace alone. Such is the state of affairs that the commands of war in Islam require a reapplication. In days gone by, kingship, whereby the ruler unilaterally possessed absolute power, was the order of the day. Now it is the age of democracy, which is another name for the politics of power sharing.

Changed situations in every age demand that efforts be made towards adaptation of the injunctions of Islam to meet new exigencies. This is the way that the Islamic shariah continues to be updated. This task of updating is performed through *ijtihad*, a process which, in any community, requires creative thinking. And the essential condition for creative thinking lies in people having full freedom of expression, including that of criticism. This is why Islam has accorded such freedom to everyone, it is in an atmosphere in which every thing and everyone is open to criticism that creativity is developed. Creative minds alone can perform the task of *ijtihad* at the highest level. Where there is no such open intellectual atmosphere, the process of mental development will come to a halt and that of updating as well.

Updating: Reapplication of Shariah

According to the Qur'an, there are two major parts of Islam—religion (*din*) and the law (*Shariah*). *Din* or *al-din* is basic and absolute, always remaining the same, without the slightest change. It is obligatory for all believers, whatever the circumstances, and entails belief in the One

God, and the worship of Him alone. The *Shariah*, on the other hand, may differ, depending upon times and places.

On the subject of *al-din* the Qur'an has this to say: He has ordained for you the same *din* which He enjoined on Nuh (Noah) and which We have revealed to you and which we enjoined on Ibrahim (Abraham) and Isa (Jesus) (saying): Observe this *din* and be not divided therein. (42:13).

On the other hand, there is another verse of the Qur'an which tells us that the shariat given to different prophets were not always identical. The Qur'an states:

> We have ordained a law *(Shariah)* and a path for each of you. And had God so willed He would have made you all a single community, but He wanted to try you by what He had given you. Vie with each other then in good works, for to God you shall all return and he will resolve for you your differences. (5:48)

The *Shariah*, or external structure of the commands of Islam, and the *minhaj*, or method varied from prophet to prophet, but only in a partial, not a total sense. It should be borne in mind also that such differences as these were related not to individual prophets but to the changed situations. The different circumstances of the times each prophet lived in were taken into account in the commands they were given in terms of the *Shariah* and *minhaj*. These variations were based on the practical wisdom rather than related to the person of a particular prophet. That is why this principle of *Shariah* is valid even today.

The principle of the change in situations governing partial and temporal alterations in the *Shariah* and *minhaj* is duly adopted . While in the past this change was carried out through the Prophet, modifications are now arrived at through *ijtihad* and carried into effect by the Islamic scholars.

That task in reality is not synonymous with bringing about a change in the *shariah* but it is only a reapplication of the shariah in terms of altered circumstances. The task of effecting such reapplication, which was undertaken in the past, will in like manner, continue to be carried out in the future. It is this process of continual adjustment which helps to keep Islam permanently updated.

Da'wah

The third requirement for this continuation of the Prophetic mission is *da'wah* work. That is, to communicate the message of the Prophet to all people in all ages.

Though this *da'wah* work is carried out by human beings, it is, in fact, a divine task. That is why the Qur'an has called it *nusrat* of God i.e., helping the Almighty (3:52).

According to the Qur'an *da'wah* work means to make oneself *nasih* and *amin*, that is, an honest and sincere well-wisher of all. (7:68).

In short, it is to become wholly honest in relation to God and to feel and evince total good will towards all one's fellow men. *Da'wah* work can be properly performed only by meeting this standard. One important condition for the performance of *da'wah* work is patience. This virtue was exemplified by the conduct of the early *da'is*: "We will exercise patience regardless of the harm inflicted upon us." (Qur'an, 14:12)

This verse of the Qur'an tells us of the character of the *da'i*. The *da'i* in relation to the *mad'u* adopts the attitude of patience unilaterally. He continues his process of *da'wah*

work in a peaceful manner despite provocation from the
other party. This is an extremely essential condition. If the
da'i is provoked by the behaviour of the madu, the normal
atmosphere between *da'i* and *mad'u* will be disturbed,—
and the whole process of *da'wah* work will be ruined. It goes
without saying that a conducive atmosphere is necessary
for the successful carrying out of *da'wah* action.

The most important aspect of this *da'wah* work is that
through it God's message continues to be communicated
to people in every age. Another aspect, no less important,
is that people from different spheres continue to enter the
fold of Islam. It is like the introduction of new blood to the
old blood into the believer. In this way the Muslim
community saves itself from the natural process of
degeneration. This is the only way of keeping the Muslim
community revitalized at all times. On the other hand, the
more the true message of Islam spreads through the *da'wah*
process around the globe, the more its textual, ideological
and practical preservation is ensured, and the more Islam
gains from the enlightenment and genius of freshly initiated
minds—a factor which will keep its teachings updated for
the generations to come.

16

✵⟨⟩✵

Islam Stands the Test of History

Islam claims to be an eternal religion. Any claim of this kind invites people to judge its validity on historical grounds. If latter day history testifies to its claim, it stands endorsed, otherwise it must be rejected. Marxism in the 20th century is a clear-cut example of historical rejection. According to his concept of historical determinism, Carl Marx held that modern industrial capitalism bore within it the seeds of its own destruction. He further observed that according to its own inherent laws its antithesis would emerge which would destroy it. Whereupon a new synthesis would come into being. But, quite contrary to his prediction, industrial capitalism has not only survived , but is making great progress. Historical events have thus buried Marxist theory. Then there is the case of Adolph Hitler who made grandiose claims that Germans were the "master race" and were destined to rule all Europe. The rout of Hitler and his Nazi party at the end of World War II put paid to all such theorizing.

But the case of Islam is quite different. Even after a period of one thousand five hundred years, Islam has suffered no erosion of its validity. The well known British historian, Edward Gibbon, describes the rise and expansion of Islam as "one of the most memorable revolutions which has impressed a new and lasting character on the nations of the globe."

An Indian historian, M.N. Roy, has observed: "Muhammad must be recognized as by far the greatest of all prophets, before or after him." He goes on to say that "the expansion of Islam is the most miraculous of all miracles." (*The Historical Role of Islam*, pp. 4-5)

The American writer, Michael Heart, in his book, "The 100" has made a selection of the 100 most influential persons in history, who have achieved the most outstanding success in this world. Right at the top of this list is the Prophet Muhammad ﷺ, of whom the author writes:

> He was the only man in history who was supremely successful on both the religious and secular levels.

The great success that the Prophet Muhammad ﷺ had predicted for his mission at the very outset exactly came true. This too, in spite of the stiff opposition which Muhammad ﷺ faced right from the beginning, both from within his own family and from the outside world. This was in 610 AD, the year when he first started receiving divine revelations. At this stage he felt totally helpless. But then, in this adverse situation, he received a revelation from God, which said:

> They want to extinguish God's light with their mouths. But God will perfect His light, even though the unbelievers may detest it. It is He who

has sent His Messenger with guidance and the
Religion of Truth, so that He may exalt it over all
religions, much as the pagans may dislike it.
(61:8-9)

At the very beginning of his prophetic career, the
Qur'an declared that Muhammad ﷺ would certainly
succeed in his mission. All his opponents, however
powerful they might be, would ultimately be defeated.
(This is pointed out at several places in the Qur'an in
different wording). In history we find numerous
personalities who began their work with towering claims,
but none of them achieved the envisioned success.
Throughout human history, the Prophet Muhammad ﷺ is
the only exception to this rule, in that his predictions were
fulfilled to the fullest extent.

Through the efforts of the Prophet and his companions,
a unique event took place: starting from scratch, they
succeeded in extending their influence to the entire
populated world of that age. During this brief period, they
not only conquered Arabia but also succeeded in crushing
the two great empires of their time—the Roman and the
Sassanid. This exceptional phase in history has been almost
universally acknowledged by historians.

The Qur'an was revealed prior to the modern age of
knowledge, yet fourteen hundred years ago, at the time of
revelation, the Qur'an declared that the proof of its being
divine in origin lay in its being in complete accordance with
historical facts and in its remaining consistent with
discoveries made contemporaneously and at all future
times. Advances may be made in human knowledge, but
they will never contradict Qur'anic statements. To a

remarkable degree, latter day history has testified to this. While many statements contained in all the ancient books have been at loggerheads with the latest scientific discoveries, the Qur'an is unique in steering clear of all such contradictions.

As the Qur'an says: "Do they not ponder on the Qur'an? had it been from other than God, they would surely have found therein much discrepancy." (4:82). (The word "discrepancy" here means inconsistency, that is, a Qur'anic statement not agreeing with eternal knowledge).

Much has been written on this aspect of the Qur'an in modern times. The French scientist, Maurice Bucaille, has shown in detail in his book, *The Bible, the Qur'an and Modern Science*, how the statements contained in the Qur'an are astonishingly in exact accordance with the discoveries of modern science. This shows that the Qur'an perfectly comes up to the scientific standards.

This development of human knowledge in favour of the Qur'anic contents is no mere accident. It is another historical proof that the Qur'an is a book revealed by the Creator of the Universe, whose knowledge is not bound by the limitations of space and time. Hence we find in the Qur'an a unique prediction to this effect:

> We will soon show them our signs in the Universe
> and in their own souls, until they clearly see that
> it is the truth. (41:53)

After completing his comparative study of the Qur'an and modern science, Maurice Bucaille comes to this conclusion:

> In view of the level of knowledge in Muhammad's
> day, it is inconceivable that many of the statements

in the Qur'an which are connected with science
could have been the work of a man. It is moreover,
perfectly legitimate, not only to regard the Qur'an
as the expression of a Revelation, but also to award
it a very special place, on account of the guarantee
of authenticity it provides and the presence in it
of scientific statements which , when studied
today, appear as a challenge to explanation in
human terms. (p. 252)

To sum up, there is no other scripture that, having
challenged all of mankind to disprove its authenticity as
the Qur'an did, finally gained total rational support for its
supernatural origin and veracity, even from its bitterest
opponents. And there is no other historic figure whose
future success was as uncertain as that of the Prophet
Muhammad, who was finally crowned with such supreme
success.

17

❦

Prophetic Vision

The Prophet Muhammad ﷺ was born in 570 in Makkah, the power centre of Arabia, and died in Madinah in 632. His father Abdullah, died prior to his birth. His mother, Amina, also died soon after his birth. There was nothing extraordinary in his external circumstances. But, from his very childhood, his personality reflected extraordinary character. On seeing him, his grandfather, Abdul Muttalib, used to remark that this grand son of his would reach a high place in life.

Chapter 93 and 94 of the Qur'an briefly describe the circumstances of his early years, and assert that, God took special care of him. In his youth when he went in search of truth, God gave him guidance through revelation. His livelihood was provided for when one of the wealthy ladies of Makkah, having become impressed by his extraordinary personality and character, desired to marry him. Besides, the Prophet was specially gifted with a vision that would enable him to recognise favourable opportunities, and turn every disadvantage to advantage.

The well known German psychologist Alfred Adler in his book, *The Individual Psychology* has written that, after studying human beings all his life, the greatest potential he found in them was "their power to turn a minus into a plus."

Throughout human history, the greatest example of this human potential coupled with vision is to be found in the Prophet Muhammad. This unique quality in him has been acknowledged by historians in diverse ways. For instance, British writer, Mr E.E. Kellet writes: "Muhammad faced adversity with the determination to wring success out of failure."

The Prophet's vision was on a totally different plane from that possessed by the common man. It would be true to say that such extraordinary vision has never been found in a person who is not a Prophet. The extraordinary nature of this vision is a proof in itself that it was not a human quality in the simple sense, but that he had received it, in a special sense, from the Almighty whose knowledge encompasses past, present and future.

As an illustration of this, we mention some incidents from the life of the Prophet. These events are not just proofs of his personal superiority but, in their essence, they also provide proof of the fact that the Prophet was an inspired person, who had received knowledge directly from God— a knowledge the acquisition of which is not possible for an ordinary man.

Envisioning the future

How great was this vision of the Prophet can be judged by an incident in the early period of his prophethood in

Makkah. It should first be explained that the Makkans regarded him as being so insignificant that instead of calling him Muhammad, son of Abdullah, they ridiculed him by calling him Muhammad the son of Abu Kabsha.' (Abu Kabsha was a shephard in Makkah, whose wife had been Muhammad's 🕌 wet nurse.) In these apparently ordinary and unpropitious circumstances, his vision was neverthless on so high a plane that, when in the early years of his prophethood, the Makkan leaders gathered at the house of Abu Talib, the Prophet's uncle, to ask the Prophet what it was that he aspired to, he replied with complete determination: I want only one word from you, if you are willing to give that, you will come to possess the whole of Arabia and all the other parts of the world will surrender before you. (*Hayat As Sahaba*, 1/56).

The day the Prophet made this pronouncement, he was all alone in the world, without a single soul to support him. To those who lacked insight he had no future, yet he could visualize something which appeared inconceivable to others. Today we all know that these words uttered by him became a part of history. Within barely twenty three years of the commencement of his mission, the whole of Arabia was brought into the fold of Islam, while in the next two decades the Roman and the Sassanid empires,— the two great empires of the world, — had surrendered before his followers. These events were so astonishing that historians have called them the greatest miracle of human history. In the words of historian M.N. Roy:

> Every Prophet established his pretension by the
> performance of miracles. By that token Muhammad
> must be recognized as by far the greatest of all

Prophets, before or after him. The expansion of
Islam is the most miraculous of all miracles.
(*Historical Role of Islam*, p.4)

Seeing an Advantage Amidst Disadvantages

After attaining to prophethood, the Prophet
Muhammad ﷺ lived in Makkah for thirteen years. This was
the most difficult period of his life: only a few of the
Makkans believed in him. While the majority—especially
the leaders—put up stiff opposition to his ideas. They
created all kinds of hardship for him and his companions,
even killing some of them; placed a total boycott on him
along with his family; deprived him of tribal protection,
and resolved to kill the Prophet himself, in order to wipe
out Islam forever etc.

In those days the circumstances appeared to be
extremely disadvantageous. It was a tribal age. It was held
that the actual power of an individual lay in his male child,
and since the Prophet had no son, his opponents used to
call him '*abtar*' (rootless), that is, he had no future. In these
apparently desperate circumstances, the Prophet replied:
"God has promised me a town which will swallow up all
other towns, people call it Yathrib, but it is Madinah."
(*Muwatta* Imam Malik, 641).

What in essence he was saying was that God had
decreed that he leave Makkah for another town, a town
which would form the centre of his mission and which
would then become so powerful as to "swallow up" all
other towns. This was a figurative way of saying that all the
nations of the world would surrender to it. This observation
appeared strange, coming as it did from one who had

become persona non grata in his own home town, Makkah, and who was now apparently living in the most straitened circumstances.

When the Prophet migrated from Makkah to Madinah, he did not even have a pair of shoes on his feet; hiding himself in this state from the Makkan leaders he reached Madinah. Called Yathrib in those days, was a town attached with no importance. However in that same Arabia where Makkah had become so inhospitable to him, Madinah proved to be quite the reverse. Almost all its inhabitants entered the fold of Islam, and moreover, the Muslims scattered outside the periphery began to settle within the town. In this way, Madinah became a powerful centre of Islam. Within the space of a few years, his mission flourished there, then it spread to all the other towns in Arabia. Ultimately, the whole of Arabia entered the fold of Islam.

Given the distressing nature of the circumstances in Makkah, it took great insight on the part of the Prophet to see what the future held for him in Madinah, which was situated at a distance of 300 miles from Makkah. The fact that he foresaw a great future there is proof of his quite remarkable vision.

Apparently, the inhabitants of both the towns, Makkah and Madinah, were idolators, yet there was a basic difference between the two: in Makkah, people's material interests were linked with idolatry, whereas, for the Madinans, idolatry was only an ancestral heritage; it had no other significance.

Due to the shortage of water in Makkah, agriculture and horticulture did not exist there. Idolatry, however, provided one of the greatest sources of the townspeople's livelihood. The Makkans had placed in the Kabah idols numbering 360, belonging to all the Arabian tribes. These Arabian tribes used to visit Kabah to worship their idols where they also offered devotional presents. Due to their visit in great numbers the business in Makkah prospered. By the visit of these devotees Makkans benefited in almost the same manner as countries benefit nowadays from the visit of tourists on a large scale. Furthermore, since the Makkans were the custodians of this idolatrous system, they had come to acquire the position of political leadership of the whole of Arabia. Abandoning idolatry, therefore, appeared to them to be synonymous with the collapse of their politics and economics.

Whereas the situation in Madinah was quite different. There was water and fertile soil. By means of agriculture and horticulture, its inhabitants easily managed to secure their livelihood. Therefore, they were not afraid that if they abandoned idolatry for monotheism, their economy would be ruined. That explains the difference in the response from the people belonging to the two cities. Where the Makkans vigorously opposed the call of monotheism given by the Prophet Muhammad ﷺ, the Madinans, soon after their first introduction to the religion of monotheism, abandoned idol worship and accepted Islam without any hesitation.

To understand this difference between Makkah and Madinah and to judge that Madinah rather than Makkah would provide the strongest ladder to progress called for keen perception. This assessment made by the Prophet Muhammad ﷺ is a living proof of the profundity of his vision, and is literally testified to by history.

Introducing Peace as the Most Powerful Weapon

The period in which the Prophet Muhammad ﷺ was born was one of war and conflict. Throughout the world the sword was regarded as the sign of power. The Arabs had a saying: The greatest check of war is war. In this connection the Prophet observed: "God grants to non-violence what he does not grant to violence." (*Al-Tirmidhi*)

In the conditions prevailing fifteen hundred years ago such observations seemed extraordinary. Such sentiments were so highly at odds with the times that words of this nature could be uttered only by one whose mind had not been moulded by his immediate circumstances, but had been inspired rather by some higher source of knowledge. Both the initial as well as the later period of Islam testify completely to the principle of inspiration.

During the life of the Prophet Muhammad ﷺ, the Quraysh, who enjoyed the leadership of Arabia, turned so hostile to him that they went to the extent of waging war against him. According to the books of *seerah*, the Quraysh wanted to embroil him in minor or major battles on more than eighty occasions. But the Prophet did his best not to engage in hostilities by adopting a peaceful policy. For instance, on the occasion of the Ahzab encounter, the Prophet set up a buffer in the form of a trench between him and his enemies. Then on the occasion of Hudaybiya, when it came to making a peace treaty with the enemy, the Prophet, accepted all the conditions set by them.

During the 23 year period of his prophethood, the Prophet, physically encountered his antagonists only on three occasions—at Badr, Uhud and Hunayn, where conflict had become totally unavoidable. Each of these three engagements lasted for only half a day. This means that the Prophet fought for only one and a half days throughout his life, with the total casualties amounting to not more than 130 from both sides. The winning over of such an aggressive and belligerent people with so little bloodshed had been possible only because the Prophet always used to lay stress on the power of peace.

Arabia had been conquered during the lifetime of the Prophet. The wars that took place in this process took a toll of less than one hundred and fifty people . This revolution brought about by the Prophet Muhammad ﷺ was indeed a bloodless revolution. And this bloodless revolution became possible only because he acted on his belief in the power of peace.

In the later centuries of Islam, too, this peace formula was followed. That is why Islam achieved such great successes. One prominent example of this matter is provided by an event which took place in the thirteenth century. During this period the barbaric Mongol tribes rose from Turkistan and devastated the entire Muslim empire right from Samarqand to Aleppo. The grand Abbasid caliphate vanished altogether.

In those days the Muslims' political and military power had so greatly weakened that the saying spread among them that if you were told that the Mongols had been defeated, you should not believe it. It was in this situation that the Islamic policy of peace performed a miracle. Muslim men and Muslim women rose to the occasion, engaging themselves in peaceful *da'wah* work. The result was miraculous, within a period of 50 years the scene was completely changed. In the words of the

Qur'an (41:34), the enemies had been turned into close friends. The majority of the Mongols had been brought into the fold of Islam.

"The Religion of Muslims had conquered where their arms had failed." (*The Preaching of Islam*, by T.W. Arnold) As another historian has put it: "The conquerors had accepted the religion of the conquered."

The Prophet Muhammad ﷺ held that the power of peace was far greater than the power of violence, and on many occasions, he and his followers successfully put this into practice. As a result this concept of peace, as opposed to violence, influenced the course of events at the time and continued to have an impact on later generations. In present times this thinking has assumed the status of a permanent social philosophy. Many prominent thinkers are its advocates. For instance, it was this principle of peaceful activism on which Mahatma Gandhi based his movement of non-violence and with this power of non-violence the freedom movement successfully achieved its target. Then it was this same principle by which the South African leader Nelson Mandela became successful in his political movement in support of the blacks against the whites.

The Prophet Muhammad ﷺ was born in the second half of the sixth century AD. It was an age of constant skirmishing. In those days people resorted to violence, regardless of the issue, for they knew of no other solution to their problems. In such an atmosphere the Prophet Muhammad ﷺ declared that the power of peace was far greater than the power of violence. This peaceful activism could have been understood only by one whose vision was so profound as to enable him to penetrate appearances in order to see reality,one of rare insight, able to penetrate the present and see the future. As we know in present times the invention and use of the latest weapons of war have only increased the destructivness of war or violence. In no way do they herald success or victory for anyone. On the other hand, advances in modern science and technology e.g. today's communications systems, have to a hitherto unimaginable extent, proved strongly supportive of the peaceful method.

These extraordinary possibilities which lay hidden in the darkness of the future fifteen hundred years ago required an exceptional vision. This observation of the Prophet serves, undoubtedly, as a vital proof of this vision.

His words determine the course of history

How extraordinary was the Prophet's declaration recorded as follows in books of *hadith*: "The chain of prophethood and messengership has been terminated and after me neither a prophet nor a messenger will be sent by God." (*Sahih Muslim*) In addition to his having said that there would be no prophet after him, this was also clearly stated in the Qur'an. (33:40).

Such a declaration had never been made before him, nor was it ever made after him. It is all the more astonishing that these words have become a matter of history. No one has so far dared to claim to be a prophet of God.

Certain personalities have been named in connection with the prophethood, but this is certainly not right. These spiritual personalities have never made a claim in clear terms such as the Prophet Muhammad did: No doubt, I am a Prophet of God. (Ibn Hisham).

The first instance in this connection is that of Musailama of Yamama (Arabia), a contemporary of the Prophet, who died in 633 AD. It is said that he claimed prophethood. But the fact is that his claim was not that of being an independent Prophet but rather of being a co-sharer in the Prophethood of Muhammad. He sent to the Prophet Muhammad ﷺ in Madinah a two member delegation who brought with them a letter from him in which it was clearly stated: "I have been made a partner in this matter of prophethood with him (Muhammad)." (*Seerat ibn Hisham*, p. 244)

This makes it evident that Musailama had never claimed independent prophethood. His claim, in fact, was that of having been appointed as a partner. This means that he himself referred the matter of prophethood to the Prophet Muhammad ﷺ himself. That is to say, that only if the Prophet Muhammad ﷺ testified to the veracity of his claim could he be held truthful. Since the Prophet did not so testify, Musailama's claim stands nullified.

Similarly, the Sikh religion is attributed to Guru Nanak, who was born in the Punjab. His devotees for their part sometimes call him a "messenger." Guru Nanak himself never claimed that he was a Prophet of God. The book, the Guru Garantha Sahab, the sacred book of Sikkhism, attributed to Guru Nanak, is actually a collection of work by different people. Nowhere in this book, is it mentioned that Guru Nanak regarded himself as God's messenger or claimed to be one. This being so, including him in the list of prophets is not worthy of consideration.

Then there is the Iranian born Bahaullah (d. 1892), who is regarded as a prophet by his followers. The religion based on his teachings is known as the Bahai faith. Now the question is 'Did he claim to be a Prophet of God?'

Events show that he never claimed either verbally or in writing to be a Prophet of God. His sole claim, according to the Bahai records, was that he was a Mahadi (Guided Person) and the manifestation of the unknowable God—*Mazhar-e-Haq*. (Eb-732).

The declaration of the Prophet Muhammad ﷺ that he was the last Prophet still remains unquestioned. The case of Bahaullah does not even figure in the list. For he never claimed to be a Prophet of God. What he claimed, rightly or wrongly, was something else, having nothing to do, directly with the declaration of the Prophet of God.

Another example is that of the India born Mirza Ghulam Ahmad Qadiani (d. 1908), regarded by some as a prophet. But, according to the historically established record, this attribution has no sanction in the works of Mirza Ghulam Ahmad Qadiani. Therefore, he cannot be included in the list of prophets for he never pronounced himself to be a Prophet of God. On the contrary what he claimed, was that he was a shadow of the Prophet Muhammad. He never projected himself as an independent Prophet. He thus left it entirely to the Prophet Muhammad either to validate or nullify his position in terms of prophethood.

As mentioned above, the Prophet Muhammad ﷺ declared that after him no Prophet or messenger would come until Doomsday. This means that after him neither a dependent nor an independent Prophet was to come to the world. The truth is that to say: "I am a Prophet" is more difficult than putting a mountain on one's head. Such words can be uttered either by one who is a Prophet of God in the real sense or by one who is insane. No third person can let this claim fall from his lips.

I have had two personal experiences in this regard, one pertains to Guru Gurbachan Singh (d.1980) and the other to Sree Karunakara Guru of Shantigiri, Trivandrum (d. May 6, 1999). The devotees of both holy men told me that their respective gurus were Prophets of God. I said that it was the guru who had the knowledge of being a Prophet of God, and not his devotees. Therefore, the question of considering such a claim seriously arose only when the concerned person uttered these words: "I am God's Prophet." So long as these words were not spoken by the concerned person, the case was not worthy of consideration.

In the case of Guru Gurbachan Singh of Delhi, chief of Nirankari mission, some of his devotees visited my office and alleged that their guru was the Prophet of the time. I said that if they believed that to be true, I would come to see their guru, and they were to ask him actually to make the assertion that he was a Prophet of God. They said that they would request their guru to do so and that he would certainly utter these words in my presence. I further added that on that occasion I shall not debate his claim. After listening to those words from the lips of the guru, I would come back without questioning it. The devotees talked to their guru, and fixed the date and the time. At the appointed hour I went to the Sant Nirankari Mandal (New Delhi), where I was ushered into the Guru's chamber. His devotees too were present along with me. Their faces showed that they were convinced that the guru would utter the desired words. I stayed with the guru for about an hour.

He continued to talk to me about his mission all this while, but he never uttered these words. For I had given my word to his devotees that I would neither question him nor enter into any debate, so after waiting for one hour, I finally left.

In the other case, that of Sree Karunakara Guru of Shantigiri, a group of his devotees came from Trivandrum to Delhi, where they visited our centre and told me that their guru was a Prophet of God. I told them that I wanted to hear these words from the lips of the Guru. They invited me to their Ashram at Shantigiri and assured me that their guru would certainly utter these words.

I went to Trivandrum in February 1999. There I met the Guru at the Shantigiri Ashram, which is located about 20 k m. away from the Trivandrum airport. This meeting took place in a spacious room, in which many of his devotees and some foreigners, men and women, were also present. These devotees were either standing or sitting on the carpet. The Guru reclined on a bed, beside which a chair was placed for me.

Thus the distance between the guru and me was about less than one meter. Since the guru did not know Hindi, the conversation took place in English. After some introductory remarks, I came to the point and asked him directly:

> Do you claim that you are a Prophet of God in the same sense in which Moses, Jesus and Muhammad claimed to be Prophets of God?

A silence fell for a few seconds after my question, then the guru replied quite clearly: "No, I make no such claim." Afterwards there was no need for further questions on this topic. I talked to him about his mission for some time, then took his leave after receiving his special parshad—an orange.

To conclude, we may confidently assert that the Prophet Muhammad ﷺ was endowed with such divine vision as enabled him to visualize the future very clearly. That is the secret behind all his religious, social and political achievements. It is no wonder then that, by the virtue of this vision, he was also able to predict the continuing ideological supremacy of his prophethood—to the extent that the history itself has refused, and will refuse credibility to any later ideological counter claims, be they made in prophetic or non-prophetic terms.

18

Islamic Activism

Addressing the Prophet Muhammad ﷺ, the Qur'an enjoins: "Therefore, bear up patiently as did the steadfast apostles before you. Bear up with patience and do not seek to hurry on their doom." (46:35)

That is, showing restraint in adverse situations and refraining from negative reaction form the basic principles of Islamic activism. This means that, in unfavourable situations, no emotional move is made; rather, by avoiding the path of reaction and retaliation, actions are planned on the basis of realism.

This principle can briefly be called positive activism. That is, without interfering with the prevailing state of affairs, one should try to discover opportunities as they occur and avail of them. To initiate one's actions by challenging the status quo amounts to choosing a negative starting point. On the other hand, maintaining the status quo and availing of all opportunities which present themselves amounts to taking a positive course of action. This method can briefly be called positive status quoism, for which a complete scheme can be chalked out in the light of the Seerah (biography) of the Prophet.

1. Positive Satatus Quoism in Religious Affairs

The Prophet Muhammad ﷺ received his first prophetic call in 610 in Makkah. This city was dominated by idolaters, who had placed in the Kabah 360 idols belonging to various Arabian tribes. The Kabah had, therefore, become a religious centre for all these tribes. The presence of these idols in the Kabah was totally against the beliefs of the Prophet, an upholder of monotheism in the true sense of the word. Yet rather than make efforts to upset the status quo in Makkah, he fully engaged himself in his task of spreading the word of God, availing of whatever opportunities were available— despite the presence of the idols.

In those days the Kabah was the gathering point of the inhabitants of Makkah, and meetings were held there almost daily. The Prophet began to make use of these gatherings for the purposes of da'wah. On his visit to the Kabah, instead of interfering with the idols, he would go to the people and recite the verses of the Qur'an to them. This policy of avoiding the idols and availing of da'wah opportunities proved to be a wise one: many people, profoundly influenced by the holy Qur'an, embraced Islam, and this without there having been any disruption of Makkah's peaceful atmosphere. This gave an added impetus to the Prophet's missionary endeavours.

2. Positive Status Quoism in Social Affairs:

In Makkah, there was a public place known as Dar Al-Nadwah, which served as a political centre. This was dominated by the idolaters. When their opposition to the Prophet Muhammad ﷺ intensified, they took a unanimous decision to boycott the Prophet, his family and his followers. When the boycott too failed to inflict any harm on his mission, his opponents issued a death warrant from this same Dar Al-Nadwa.

When the Prophet heard of this, although his situation was now extremely serious, he did not attempt either to revoke the decision of Dar al-Nadwa or to launch a protest campaign supported by his followers. On the contrary, what the Prophet did was quietly leave the city for Madinah, a town 300 miles away from Makkah. Even after reaching Madinah, he did not devote any time to planning counter moves, but gave his full attention to the task of *da'wah*. This was also an example of positive status quoism. In this way, the Prophet, by avoiding direct confrontation with the situation at hand, found another vast field in which to continue his peaceful activities.

3. Positive Status Quoism in Political Affairs:

When the Prophet migrated to Madinah, after thirteen years of his prophethood, the existing society of Madinah was composed of three groups—Muslims, idolaters, and Jews. Accepting that social set-up as it was, the Prophet established a system based on plurality. The status of Madinah under this system was that of a city state, the Prophet being the head of state. Within this framework other social groups were granted the right to lead their lives as they wished and resolve their issues in accordance with their respective religions and cultures.

This set-up provided another example of status quoism. It was by accepting the prevailing situation there that the

Prophet began his peaceful *da'wah* mission. The result was miraculous. The multi-cultural society of the first phase was gradually transformed into a unicultural society in the second phase.

4. Positive Status Quoism in Matters Relating to Prestige:

Even after the Prophet's departure from Makkah —his homeland—for Madinah, the Makkans, unflagging in their enmity, decided to launch an armed onslaught against him. Apart from several minor skirmishes, two major battles, Badr and Uhud, took place. These wars again disturbed the peaceful atmosphere required to carry out *da'wah* activities. Therefore the Prophet negotiated with the Makkans and, accepting all their demands unilaterally, entered into a 10-year no-war pact, known as the Hudaybiyyah treaty. This was yet another example of positive status quoism. By the terms of this treaty the Prophet accepted the Makkan position exactly in accordance with their demands. By his acceding to their position, the Prophet was able to utilize all the opportunities for *da'wah* work offered by the situation. This resulted in what the Qur'an called an 'open victory.' (48:24)

5. Positive Status Quoism in Post Related Affairs:

Throughout a significant part of his life, Muhammad ﷺ was a messenger of God as well as the head *of* state. After his death the question arose as to who should be chosen to fill the latter position. This issue was settled by following the guideline given by the Prophet: "The head of state will be selected from amongst the Quraysh."

Ostensibly, it was an unusual injunction, for, according to the teachings of Islam, all human beings are equal. None enjoys any superiority over another. As such this advice to select the leader from amongst the Quraysh was a form of discrimination. But it was realistic rather than discriminatory. This was another example of positive status quoism. In fact, over the centuries, in line with ancient traditions, the Quraysh had acquired the position of leadership in Arabia. A sudden change in this status quo would therefore have created insurmountable problems. That was why the Prophet advised the Muslims to accept the existing political system. As a result of this wise policy, Arab unity remained intact and the furtherance of the Islamic mission continued unhampered, even after the death of the Prophet.

6. Positive Status Quoism in State Affairs:

Even after the demise of the Prophet Muhammad ﷺ, this practice of positive status quoism continued in the early phase of Islam. One outstanding example is the policy adopted by the religious scholars during the latter half of the Umayyad period and the entire Abbasid era. The political system had been corrupted during this period. Yet almost all the great Muslim scholars of those times (ulama, traditionists, jurists) avoided setting themselves on a collision course with those in authority. The religious scholars were thus saved from the backlash of the Muslim rulers; while those who, opted for the course of confrontation with the rulers were removed from the scene.

This policy of non-interference in the political system left scholars free to produce that great treasure known as the library of Islam. It is a historical fact that almost the entire classical Islamic literature was prepared during this period. The development of the Arabic language, its grammar, its calligraphy, the exegesis of the Qur'an, the collection and editing of the *hadith*, the formulation of civil and religious laws (*fiqh*), the preparation of the literature of *kalam* (theology), etc.— all were developed during this period.

It is a fact that, had the Muslim scholars and *ulama* of the age risen against a political system which they held to be corrupt, all this precious literature would never have come into existence, and the major part of the *hadith*, which enjoys the status of the second source in Islam, would not have been safely transferred to succeeding generations. The age of the press had not yet dawned, and the sole repositories of all Islam's spiritual riches were the memories of the surviving scholars. Had these scholars engaged themselves in political confrontations with the rulers, all the treasures of Islamic thought and practice would have been buried along with them.

In social matters, positive status quoism is thus an unalterable policy of Islam. It was by opting for this policy that the Prophet and his companions forged the great history of Islam which heralded a new era in all the religious and secular fields of human civilization.

Unlimited Scope of Patience

When the Prophet Muhammad ﷺ began his mission of *tawhid* (unity of God) in ancient Makkah, there existed as usual a status quo. The Quraysh had assumed the leadership of the town, and according to their beliefs, they had established an idolatrous system. Now the question arose as to how the Prophet Muhammad ﷺ should begin his work. It appeared that the status quo under the hegemony of the Quraysh would have to be abolished and only then would the path be cleared for Prophet's mission. At that juncture, certain basic guidance was revealed to the Prophet. God declared in the Qur'an:

Surely with every hardship there is ease; with every hardship there is surely ease. (94:5-6)

This means that although the status quo in Makkah appeared to be an obstacle, by the very law of nature, opportunities for the furtherance of his aims opportunities also existed side by side. Therefore, any attempt to change the status quo was not to be made in the first stage itself. Without disturbing the prevailing situation such opportunities as were available in other fields were to be utilized to promote the Islamic mission.

The method Islam prescribes for the achievement of our goals, and the model example we find in the life of the Prophet, can be described, in brief, as a method based on patience. That is, remaining in harmony with the status quo and launching one's struggle in the sphere of the possible. In this respect, it may be called positive status quoism.

1. An Obstacle Turned Into a Stepping Stone:

When the Prophet Muhammad ﷺ began his mission in Makkah, hundreds of idols had been placed in the most sacred mosque. The Kabah, which was built as a centre of monotheism, had virtually become a centre of shirk (polytheism). At that time the method adopted by the Prophet Muhammad ﷺ provides a perfect example of Positive status quoism.

What the Prophet Muhammad ﷺ did was to refrain completely from interfering with the idols and idol worship.

Instead, letting things remain as they were, the Prophet began to communicate the call of monotheism to the people who used to visit the Kabah daily, it being a central place. The Prophet availed of these large gatherings by going there every day and reading out to them passages from the Qur'an. In this way Islam began to spread gradually in the country.

2. *Avoidance of Protest Gradually Changes the Status Quo:*

The Prophet lived in Makkah for thirteen years after he received his prophethood. During this period, a group of people embraced Islam, but the majority continued to be diametrically opposed to it.

At that time in Makkah, Dar-al-Nadwa was its political centre. The Makkan leaders held meetings here and decided unanimously to boycott the Prophet Muhammad ﷺ. When they failed to apply a brake even with this method, they decided to assassinate him. At that time, the Prophet Muhammad ﷺ did not launch a campaign to capture Dar-al-Nadwa, the centre of his opposition. The Prophet did not even commence hostilities against these Makkan leaders. There was no fight to the finish. Instead what he did once again was to accept the status quo and quietly leave that place for Madinah, which became the centre of his activities. As history tells us, extraordinary results were produced through this superb and far-sighted strategy.

3. *Internal Harmony Results in External Expansion:*

At that time in Madinah, three religious groups existed—Muslims, Idolators and Jews. Here too the Prophet Muhammad ﷺ did not directly confront the status quo. Instead, he issued a charter which is known as Sahifa-al-

Madinah in the history of Islam. In this situation he adopted almost the same kind of policy as that known as non-interference in modern times. He declared that every religious group would enjoy full freedom in religious and cultural matters, and that the systems in Madinah will be run on the basis of the policy of mutual respect.

Consequently, the Prophet found an opportunity to consolidate his mission without unnecessarily setting himself on a collision course. Even after he had left his homeland, the Makkans did not leave him alone. They continued their hostile activities against him. Many big and small battles took place as a result.

Again the Prophet followed the same policy of refraining from interfering with the status quo. By accepting the superior position of the Makkans he entered into a peace treaty with them, which is known as the Hudaybiyya Peace Treaty. In this, he acknowledged the established position of the Makkans and made a truce with the condition that no war would take place between the two parties for a period of ten years. The Hudaybiyya Peace Treaty was a successful example of positive status quoism. Consequently, the Prophet, by accepting the prevalent situation in Arabia, secured full opportunities for peaceful *da'wah* struggle and this opened the door for a "clear victory" in the words of the Qur'an (48:24). The principle of Islamic activism has been briefly alluded to in the Qur'an:

> Therefore bear up patiently as did the steadfast
> prophets before you. Bear up with patience and do
> not seek to hurry on their doom. (46:35).

According to this verse, there were in any given situation two ways of launching a campaign,— the patient and the impatient.

The latter is that of emotional while the former is that of considered response. The impatient person launches himself on a collision course at the very outset making the continuance of the struggle impossible. On the contrary, one who follows the patient method, and avoids any confrontation with the status quo, is free to make full use of any opportunities which come his way. This method leads to sure success without creating any new problems in society.

In short, there is unlimited scope for both individuals and groups who adopt the patient method as a matter of permanent policy in all their affairs. In this lies the secret of all great successes. This course of positive status quoism ensures that all our powers and potential will be completely focussed on the accomplishment of long term constructive plans, rather than being unnecessarily wasted in any non-productive or even self-destructive activity against the status quo.

Moreover, if you are one of those who wish to work for Islam or struggle for the revival of the Muslim Ummah, then treading the path of patience and adhering to the principle of positive status quoism is strictly obligatory on you. Firstly as we have shown earlier, it has been highly recommended in the Qur'an, and secondly, it was by the application of this same method that Islam secured an unopposed victory over all its enemies, bringing into existence, as a result, the ideal Muslim society of the early period of Islam.

19

The Islamic Concept of History

According to the Qur'an, God has created the universe with a certain purpose, and all its parts which are strictly under His control, are carrying out His divine scheme without the slightest deviation. Similarly, man too has been created with a certain purpose. Yet man, on the contrary, is totally free. He can do what he wants by his own decision. However, in spite of this freedom he is being watched constantly by God, for He does not allow any such deviation in human history over a long period as would nullify His very creation plan.

Creation Plan of God

The Universe made by God is so vast that, despite the enormous progress made by human beings in their attempts to fathom the universe, many of its secrets still remain unknown. The planet earth, made by God as part of the cosmos was and still is unique in the entire universe, in that it has been endowed with an atmosphere and all the other factors which are essential to make it habitable for man.

After bringing into existence a favourable world in the form of the earth, God created the first man Adam and his feminine counterpart, Eve. Although the precise date of this event is unknown, it is a fact that the first pair of human beings to set foot on earth was this very Adam and Eve.

Adam was the first man as well as the first Prophet. The way of God is to select a man as His messenger from amongst human beings themselves in order to send His revelations to mankind. Therefore, God revealed to Adam through an angel the purpose of man's inhabiting the earth. According to this plan, God created a creature in the form of man, upon whom He bestowed freedom. Where the rest of the universe had no choice but to submit to the will of God, it is desirable for man to opt for this divine plan of his own free will.

This plan of divine will is based on two basic principles—monotheism and justice. Monotheism holds man to worshipping one God alone, and not associating anyone or anything in this worship. Justice holds man to adhering completely to ethical principles in dealing with other human beings and refraining from all kinds of injustice and oppression.

Along with this, God informed man that, although he appeared to be free, he was fully accountable to Him. God had a complete record of man's actions. In the eternal life after death God would judge everyone according to this record. One who exercised his freedom wrongly would be thrown into eternal hellfire.

Adam prepared tablets of clay on which he engraved the basic divine teachings, then heated them in a fire, thus preserving this divine guidance for the coming generations.

It is believed that these divine teachings were written by Adam in the Syriac language.

Adam died at a ripe old age. For a long period of time his people continued to adher faithfully to the divine guidance. But later rot began to set in in the people. Idolatry replaced monotheism. People began to adopt the ways of injustice and oppression instead of justice and rectitude. After about one thousand years the perversion became so all pervading that they were completely distanced from the path of the Shariah as shown by Adam.

The Age of Perversion

God subsequently sent Noah as His messenger. He was granted an exceptionally long life of nine hundred and fifty years. During this extended period, he continued to show people the right path, generation after generation. But only a few people heeded his words. The rest persisted in their sinful ways. Then, in accordance with the ways of God, a huge flood engulfed them by way of punishment. Noah and his small band of followers were saved in a boat, while all the rest were drowned.

At that time, human population was probably concentrated only in the region of Asia known as Mesopotamia. The men and women saved in the wake of this flood settled afterwards in other parts of the world. Their race multiplied until it spread over the three continents of Asia, Africa and Europe.

After the death of Noah, his people continued for a considerable time to adhere to the divine path shown by him. But again rot set in in later generations and they again deviated from the path of monotheism as well as of justice.

God's messengers—the Qur'an has mentioned twenty six
by name—continued to come for several thousand years.
The Hadith tell us that about one hundred thousand
messengers came to the world. In this way a long period
elapsed between Adam and Messiah, when God's
messengers continued to come to the world in almost every
generation. But each time only a few individuals believed
in them. The majority rejected these prophets in every age.

The Reasons for Perversion

What were the reasons for this continued transgression?
There were two main reasons; one, political absolutism;
another, ignorance about the world of nature.

In ancient times the system of monarchy prevailed
everywhere. The kings of those days had adopted an easy
strategy for the consolidation of their empire, and that was
to apply a complete curb on intellectual freedom. As a
result, science could not make any progress in the days
of old.

The same was the case with religion. The policy
adopted by these kings was not to allow their subjects to
follow any religion other than that approved of by the king.
Superstitious religion served their purpose only too well.
Therefore, not only did they themselves embrace
superstitious religion but they also compelled their subjects
to adhere to it. People were denied the right to think freely
and opt for any religion other than the official one. This
policy of the kings produced the evil of religious
persecution. History shows that religious persecution has
continued from time immemorial in one form or another.

The other main factor in this connection was ignorance.

In ancient times man knew too little about the world and its phenomena. Political absolutism had placed an almost total ban on scientific research. Therefore, all kinds of superstitions regarding natural phenomena made inroads unchecked. It was generally held that the sun, the moon and the stars etc. possessed supernatural powers. Similarly it was believed that the sea, the mountains and other such natural phenomena were endowed with some extraordinary, mysterious power and exercised decisive control over human destiny.

The Problem of Evil

Those who want to interpret human history in the light of predetermined law as is done in the physical world, cannot but meet with failure. While the physical world may be explainable within the framework of predeterminism, the events of the human world are simply not amenable to interpretation in terms of any such law.

Others want to interpret the events of the human world in the context of freedom. But they are not satisfied either with their interpretation. This is because in the case of human freedom, the suffering experienced in this world has no valid understandable explanation. The failure of both these interpretations is due to the fact that they attempt to explain the whole in the light of a part—which is not at all possible.

The truth is that the right principle by which to interpret human history is neither that of predeterminism nor of freedom. According to Islam, there is only one correct principle to interpret human history and that is the principle of test. Man has been placed in the present world for the purpose of being tested. On the outcome of this test will depend the eternal future of all mankind.

Favourable circumstances were a sine qua non for this test in the world. Predeterminism had to a certain extent to be a feature of these circumstances as a guarantee against any obstacle coming in the way of carrying out man's trial. On the other hand, the element of freedom was also essential in order that the intentions and actions of each individual could be properly judged. For man can be granted the credit for a good deed only on the condition that, despite having the opportunity to indulge in bad deeds, he chooses of his own free will to act virtuously.

If in this world everything had been totally predetermined, the element of trial would have been absent. However the granting of freedom did involve the risk of some people misusing their freedom and misuse it they did. This gave rise to the problem of human suffering which results from evil, yet this suffering, or evil, is a very small price to pay for a very precious thing. According to Islam that person is most precious who leads his life in this world in such a manner that despite facing all sorts of temptations he succeeds in overcoming them. Despite having the power to misuse his freedom, he refrains from doing so. Despite the possibility of leading an unprincipled life, he chooses of his own free will to be a man of principle. To identify such individuals, it is essential that an atmosphere of freedom prevail in the world. This is not possible under any other system.

20

※〜(ご)〜※

The Revolutionary Role of Islam

As a result of ignorance the evil known as the worship of natural phenomena was born in human society. Man attributed divinity to mere creatures. He began to worship all the things in the world, holding them to be gods. Owing to this intellectual aberration, idolatry became a rooted feature of human civilization. Not even the coming of thousands of Prophets and reformers could bring about any change in this state of affairs, in the practical sense. The rejection of the Prophets brought down on the deniers the chastisement of God, but *shirk* could never be wiped out from society. Then God took it upon Himself to intervene. One major manifestetion of this divine intervention in human history was the emergence of the Prophet Muhammad. An American encyclopaedia has very appropriately described his coming as having "changed the course of human history."

French historian, Henri Pirenne, has expressed it thus: "Islam changed the face of the globe. The traditional order of history was overthrown."

The Qur'an, in defining the objective of the divine intervention, has this to say:

> It is He that has sent forth His Prophet with
> guidance and the true faith, so that he may exalt
> it above all religions. God is the All-sufficient
> witness (48:28).

This has found expression in a *hadith* recorded in Sahih al-Bukhari:

> He will not depart from this world as God has
> decreed, unless and until these people are brought
> to the straight path. (*Fathul Bari* 449-8).

This shows that, for the prophets of the past, communication alone was required, whereas for the Prophet Muhammad ﷺ, not just communication but also implementation was required.

The task of the earlier prophets was completed with the full communication of the message to the people. But the divine plan in sending the Prophet Muhammad ﷺ to the world was to bring about a practical revolution. His message could not, therefore, remain at the theoretical stage.

It being beyond human capacity to make the end result a certainty, how was the Prophet's message to be translated into reality? It all became possible due to the special divine succour extended to the Prophet by God. This took the form of a divine plan which had two basic aspects to it: one, to provide the Prophet with a powerful and trustworthy team, and the other to significantly weaken the enemies of monotheism by means of a special strategy, so that the Prophet and his companions could easily dominate their opponents.

The first part of this divine plan was brought to completion in the form of the settlement of Ismail, son of Prophet Ibrahim, in the unpopulated desert of Arabia two thousand five hundred years ago. At that time it was a totally isolated place situated far from the centres of civilization. There a community was raised by Ismail ibn Ibrahim, trained in the desert atmosphere where there was nothing save nature. As a natural result of this unadulterated atmosphere, (free from all man-made pollution,) the human qualities of the inhabitants of the desert were fully preserved. It was like a vast natural training camp. It took more than two thousand years to evolve a nation of such high calibre as to be called a "nation of heroes" by a western scholar. In the history of the Arabs this nation is known as the Ismailites. Despite religious perversion having set in, so distinguished were they in human values—thanks to their particular training—that they had no peers among those who came before or after them.

The Prophet Muhammad ﷺ, one of the distinguished members of the Banu Ismail, struggled for about thirteen years in Makkah and ten years in Madinah. Ultimately, more than one hundred thousand people believed in him and joined his mission. Each and every one of his companions possessed a strong and dependable character. In this way the Prophet Muhammad ﷺ, in an exceptional way, secured a team by which he could bring the message of the prophets to fruition—taking the prophetic mission from the theoretical stage of ideology to the practical stage of revolution.

The next part of this divine plan consisted of weakening these anti-monotheism forces so considerably that the last

Prophet might subjugate them and usher in the desired revolution in the very first generation itself. To achieve this end, the Arabian tribes remained engaged for a long period of time in bloody, internecine warfare. Consequently, when the Prophet Muhammad ﷺ was sent to the world, the idolatrous tribes of Arabia, having so weakened themselves, could not continue their resistance for long. This enabled the Prophet Muhammad ﷺ to overcome Arabia and root out idolatry completely within a short period of time.

In those days there were two great empires outside of Arabia. These empires kept the major parts of Asia and Africa under their full control. Their power was so great that the Arabs could not even have dreamed of overcoming them. Despite this extremely out of proportion difference, how did it become possible for the Arabs of the very first generation, to conquer both these empires—the Sassanid and Roman—in such a decisive way as to crush them absolutely, resulting in the dominance of monotheism over idolatry throughout this region? This miracle became a reality owing to a special divine strategy, which is paralleled by the case of the Romans:

> The Romans have been defeated in a neighbouring
> land. But after their defeat they shall themselves
> gain victory within a few years. (Qur'an, 30:1-3)

History shows that from 602 to 628, extremely extraordinary events took place between these two great empires.

First, the royal families in the respective countries clashed internally with one another, and in consequence, many individuals of great political worth were killed. In fact, these feuds gave a death blow to these empires, shaking them to the very roots. Subsequently, certain factors led to the destructive collision of these empires with one another. First the armies of the Sassanid empire crossed the border of the Roman empire to attack it. Circumstances proved favourable and they succeeded to the extent that the Roman Emperor Heraclius decided to flee from his Palace in Constantinople. But again, events took a new turn. Heraclius regained his lost confidence and after making full preparations, attacked the Sassanid empire, destroyed their armed forces and penetrated right into the heart of Jerusalem.

These civil wars, lasting for about twenty five years, considerably weakened both these empires. Therefore, during the pious caliphate when the Arab forces entered the Roman and Sassanid empires, they managed to advance with great speed.

Historical Revolution

This expansion of the Islamic empire was not simply a political event. Its aim, in fact, was to set in motion a revolutionary process in history. This process had been initiated in Makkah itself, then it travelled from Makkah to Madinah, to Damascus and Baghdad from where it entered Spain and thereafter it spread all over Europe and the entire world. We would probably be right in saying that the 20th century saw the culmination of this process.

There are two basic aspects to this movement. One was the end of religious persecution. (This kind of persecution has been mentioned in the Qur'an as 'fitna'). (8:39)

The process began with the end of idolatry and was completed during the lifetime of the Prophet. The other, the advent of religious freedom, came about later, during the pious caliphate; with the disintegration of the two great empires—the Sassanid and Byzantine—the two greatest pillars of religious persecution were uprooted, and religious freedom became the order of the day. However, no great revolution materialises all of a sudden. It reaches fruition only by a long historical process, and the Islamic revolution was no exception to this rule. The process of human liberation, initiated by Islam, continued over a long period to make advances through individual and collective efforts, taking various forms. The second Caliph, Umar Faruq (d.644) addressing one of his governors and his son in a well known case asked: "Since when have you enslaved people while their mothers had given birth to them in freedom?" (*Al-Abqariat Al-Islamia*).

This voice was echoed eleven hundred years later by the well known French reformer Rousseau (d. 1778). His book, titled *The Social Contract*, began with this famous sentence: ' Man was born free, but I find him in chains. This concept of intellectual and religious freedom had fully matured by the end of the 20th century. With the establishment of the United Nations all the nations of the world signed its charter of Human Rights, proclaiming that intellectual and religious freedom is the irrevocable right of every human being and that on no pretext can it be abrogated.

Freedom of Choice

Through a long process, that age has finally come when man has secured the absolute right to adopt the religion of his choice and to propagate that religion, on the sole condition that he will not use violence in the exercise of his religious freedom. This change brought about in the world has thrown open all the doors of communication formerly locked to the message of monotheism; doors that had been locked by the ancient absolutist regimes.

The creation plan of God regarding human beings has been thus alluded to in the Qur'an: "He created death and life, so that He might try which of you is best in deed." (67:2).

To achieve this end, it is essential that an atmosphere of freedom prevail in this world, that everyone without any hindrance may play his role. Without freedom, neither reward nor punishment can be awarded to anyone. An atmosphere where there is no intellectual freedom nullifies the very scheme of God—the scheme according to which man has been created and placed in this world. That is why these regimes based on an absolutism, which had taken root centuries ago, had to be overthrown.

In recent times the communist revolution of 1917 again attempted to establish a vast empire based on the coercive system of the ancient type. But since this ran counter to the divine plan, God brought about a situation which lead to the collapse of the Soviet Union in 1991. Man again was granted the same freedom as was available to the rest of the world.

The end of the superstitious Era

Another basic change wrought by the Islamic revolution was similar in some respects to the scientific revolution of modern times; that is, the rooting out of superstitious thinking on scientific grounds and the general prevalence of thinking based on facts.

As mentioned above, the continued existence of the idolatrous way of life and thinking in ancient times was due to the ignorance of human beings regarding nature. Ancient man used to judge natural phenomena by their appearance. Holding them sacred, he began to worship them. For the first time in human history, Islam succeeded in convincing people that these phenomena of nature were not creators, but only creatures. They were entirely helpless beings, mere slaves and not the masters of man.

In the wake of this revolution, the ideological base of idolatry was wiped out altogether. All those things held sacred were relegated to the status of mere creatures. They were there to be harnessed by man and not for man to be enslaved by them. The sun was held to be a god and worshipped in ancient times; the man of today is converting the sun into solar energy. Ancient man held the moon sacred; modern man has set his foot on it. Ancient man had deified the river; modern man has converted rivers into steam power, etc.

In this way, it has happened for the first time in human history that the phenomena of nature, looked upon by ancient man with reverence, have now become objects of investigation. In other words, Islam started the process of scientific enquiry. The Qur'an repeatedly enjoins man to reflect on the objects of the universe. This is no simple matter. The act of pondering over the nature of the phenomena of the universe has been accorded the status of worship in Islam. As a result of this thinking, for the first time in known history, all things in the universe have been subjected to research and investigation.

The scientific way of thinking of the modern age initiated in the early period of Islam, continued as a process to grow, spreading from one country to another until it reached the west where it saw its culmination in the western world. In respect of its reality, this scientific thinking is a revolution desirable by Islam itself.

After this revolution for the first time in human history the idolatrous way of thinking has been totally deprived of its ideological base. The concept of the sacredness of natural phenomena is now seen for what it is—a superstition, for modern scientific investigation has demonstrated belief of this kind to be baseless.

All that happened was exactly in accordance with the divine plan, the Prophet and his companions having been asked to carry out this divine scheme: "Fight them until there be no persecution and religion be wholly God's." (8:39) This means that there was no longer any barrier to man's making a choice in the way of God.

This was the final goal of the revolution brought about by the Prophet Muhammad ﷺ and his companions. It ended that absolutist system of coercion which places curbs upon personal decisions about one's religion. It also removed the veil of obstacles in ideological terms which confused and mislead people, as a result of which they began to worship creatures supposing them to be creators. (For further details see the author's book, *Islam: the Creator of the Modern Age*).

The Qur'an tells us that there is no compulsion in the matter of religion, with the proviso that true guidance and misconceptions should be thoroughly separated from one another. (2:256).

Truth and falsehood stand clearly separated from each other, just like light and darkness after the sun has risen. This was something which—after the Islamic revolution—could be grasped beyond the shadow of a doubt by anyone who sought reality with an open mind. No one was left groping in the dark. And no one was left with any excuses for rejecting God.

Truth Unveiled

To this particular end God brought about the revolutions in human history, as mentioned above. Now truth and untruth have become so distinct from one another that there is no thick or thin veil in between: the task of clarification has been performed so thoroughly that the man of today has total freedom of choice. Now in his journey towards God, man is hindered neither by false ideologies nor by practical barriers.

21

✺⟪҉⟫✺

Islam in History

According to a tradition, the Prophet Muhammad ﷺ observed that every verse of the Qur'an has two levels of meaning, one apparent and one hidden. That is, we have to read between the lines in order to go beyond the literal meaning and then, by keener concentration, arrive at its deeper significance.

So far as the literal import of the Qur'an is concerned, this was fully understood by the people at the time of revelation itself. For instance, the verse, 'Say, God is one,' (Qur'an, 112:1) was correctly construed by the Muslims of the early period of Islam, just as it will be today. There will be no difference in meaning with the passage of time. But, on more profound reflection, Qur'anic nuances, hidden in the lines, become unveiled. Such close study is engaged in in every period of time, so that new shades of meaning will continue to be revealed in every age.

According to a *hadith*, the Prophet Muhammad ﷺ observed: "The wonders of the Qur'an will never come to an end." (*Mishkat al-Masabih*, Vol. 1, p. 659). This *hadith* refers to that aspect of the Qur'an which is of deeper significance, or that which lies between the lines. The Qur'an being the scriptures of an eternal religion, new connotations will go on being revealed in every succeeding age as a result of profound reflection. This process will continue uninterrupted until Doomsday.

Here I should like to focus on certain very apt verses appearing at two places in the Qur'an. (2:193, 8:39). They concern *qital-e-fitna*, that is, the abolition of religious persecution. When we study these verses in the light of other related verses of the Qur'an, we find that it was God's plan to abolish religious persecution and replace it with complete religious freedom, so that His servants could worship Him alone without any fear of persecution. Along with that, the door to the call of monotheism also was to be thrown wide open.

The Eradication of Fitna

Islam emerged in the first quarter of the seventh century. At that time, monarchy was the order of the day all over the world. To the political rulers of that epoch, dissent of any kind, particularly religious free thinking, was anathema, because they saw it as a threat to their power. Therefore, to achieve political consolidation, the monarchs of those days adopted the principle of ideological coercion. Religious persecution thus became a weapon in the hands of the despots, so that no new ideology could be allowed to develop. Strong exception was taken to the growth of any other religion save that approved by the state. The independent thinking so essential for intellectual progress, was thus cruelly suppressed, and that was why, during the long periods of monarchical rule, neither could the sciences flourish, nor could individuals opt for the religion of their choice. Anyone who had the audacity to make an issue of this was likely to face summary execution.

The Qur'an refers thus to the religious oppression of ancient times:

> Cursed be the people of the trench, who lighted the consuming fire and who sat around it watching the believers whom they were torturing. And they had nothing against them, save that they believed in God, the Mighty, the Praiseworthy. (85:4-8)

The human condition of those days is similarly depicted in a Makkan tradition narrated by Khabbab ibn al Arat: We complained to the Prophet at a time when he was resting in the shade of the Kabah wall. We said to him: "Don't you pray for us to God?" The Prophet replied: "Those who went before you faced such unbearable trials (due to their faith in a religion other than that of the state). One of them would be brought for trial, a pit would be dug for him, then he would be buried in it in a standing posture, with his head above the edge of the pit. Then a saw would be passed through his head until it split into two parts. Yet even such severe trials did not cause him to waver from his faith. People were scraped with iron combs until all their skin came off and the bones of their bodies were exposed. Yet these acts of persecution did not deter them from adhering to their faith. Certainly God's will shall prevail (that is, the age of religious freedom will certainly come) when a traveller will journey from Sana'a to Hadhramawt, (that is, from one region to another,) without fearing anyone save God. And he will fear no wolf for his sheep. Yet you are in a hurry." (*Sahih Bukhari, Kitab al-Manaqib,* Chapter, *Alamaat an Nubuwah fi'l Islam*).

This *hadith* shows that one of the revolutionary changes to be ushered in in the wake of the Prophet's mission was the end of this ancient age of religious persecution and the replacing of it with an age of religious freedom in order to smooth the path for God's servants to follow His religion. This most significant transformation was to take place as part of a divine plan. That is why the Qur'an enjoined the Prophet's companions to pray in advance to God: "Lord, do not lay on us the burden you laid on those before us. Lord, do not charge us with more than we can bear." (2:286)

This prayer was revealed by God Himself for the benefit of the believers. It was like a divine ordinance announced in the form of a prayer to be recited by the companions. This means that God, who is the controller of history, had decreed a change in this coercive political system of ancient times in order that the religion of Monotheism could be practised and the invitation to people to answer its call could be issued in an atmosphere of freedom—a task which till that point had been seriously hindered by the prevalent religious oppression.

This divine edict became a reality, ostensibly as a result of human intervention, but actually with the succour of the Almighty. In consonance with this divine plan, the Qur'an enjoined the believer to "make war on them until persecution (*fitna*) shall cease and Religion is only for God. If they desist, God is cognizant of all their actions; but if they pay no heed, know then that God will protect you. He is the Noblest Helper and Protector." (8:39-40).

Religious coercion through persecution was totally

against the Creation Plan of God. God created this world for the purpose of putting mankind to the test. For this purpose to be fulfilled, everyone in this world had to enjoy full freedom of speech and action. If people were divested of their freedom, the very purpose of the test would be defeated. Therefore, God granted special help to the believers, so that they might put an end to a system which had suppressed the freedom essential to the divine test in this world.

In order that religion might be wholly for God, the original natural state had to be re-established, that is, a state which was in accordance with the creation plan of God. Here religion (*din*) does not refer to Shariah, but to what in chapter 30, verse 30 of the Qur'an is called 'upright nature.' That is to say, what the believers were commanded to establish was religion in the sense of divine nature and not religion in the sense of Shariah. In other words, it would be proper to say that it was like a kind of divine operation carried out by the Prophet's companions. This was initiated in Arabia where, within a period of 23 years, the religious oppression which had prevailed there under the Quraysh, was brought to an end forever.

In those days, there were two great powers in the neighbourhood of Arabia—the Sassanid and the Byzantine empires. These were two of the greatest bastions of the politically coercive system of ancient times. Their perpetuation meant the consolidation of this manner of governance and it was only their extinction which could put an end to it. However the believers launched these campaigns against the empires in defence. The aggression had been initiated by these empires themselves. This oppression soon bore fruit during the rule of the second caliph, Umar Faruq. During his caliphate, the light of these two despotic empires was forever extinguished.

The French historian, Henri Pirenne, has rightly observed that, if the Arab Muslims of the seventh century had not liquidated the Sassanid and Byzantine empires, mankind might never have been freed from tyranny, and the world might never perhaps have witnessed the age of human freedom with its sweeping intellectual revolution.

Abdullah ibn Umar, a companion of the Prophet Muhammad 鑿 and son of the second caliph, observed on one occasion: "we fought according to the Qur'anic injunction to end fitna, religious persecution, until fitna was abolished from the face of the earth forever." (*Sahih al-Bukhari*).

This means that *fitna*, or the ancient political coercive system, had been dealt a severe blow during the period of the pious caliphate itself but, like many other major historical revolutions, this new phase only very gradually reached its culmination.

In the wake of the revolution in the first phase of Islam, religious freedom took a decisive course in history, spurred on in the initial stages by Muslim action, and in the later stages by the active participation of non-Muslim nations. In the first half of the twentieth century, firstly through the League of Nations and later through the United Nations, all the nations of the world unanimously declared that religious freedom was a fundamental right for all, and could not under any circumstances be abrogated.

The Age of Religious Freedom

The first stage of the cessation of *fitna*, which brought with it the dawn of religious freedom, was accomplished in Arabia. This development took place during the lifetime of the Prophet. During his last days, on the occasion of his final Hajj, the Prophet Muhammad ﷺ preached a sermon, generally known as the Sermon of the Last Pilgrimage, in the presence of all of his companions. One of the points in his address on which the Prophet laid emphasis was that God had sent him "as a mercy to all mankind," and that this being so, they should communicate this message of peace to all people everywhere. In obedience to this injunction given by the Prophet towards the end of his life, his companions travelled far and wide beyond the boundaries of Arabia. Indeed, they spent the rest of their lives carrying out their Prophet's command. Thereafter, their successors, as well as the disciples of these successors, continued to make it their mission to disseminate the teachings of Islam, to the point where finally, the message of Islam had reached the greater part of the known, inhabited world of that age. This *da'wah* process, from beginning to end, was carried out in an entirely peaceful manner. The mere introduction of the ideology of Islam was sufficient to conquer the hearts of the people. British historian, Sir Arthur Keith writes of the Egyptians:

> The Egyptians were conquered not by the Sword
> but by the Qur'an.

This is true not only of the Egyptians, but also of all other nations which entered the fold of Islam. A detailed account of this peaceful spread of God's religion is given in *The Preaching of Islam*, by British historian, T.W. Arnold. This work, running to 508 pages, was first published in 1896. In this matter, the policy of Islam is to keep political activity separate and at a distance from the task of propagation, in order that the communication of the divine message may continue unhampered. Wherever there is political power, the element of coercion cannot be far away: political confrontations must, therefore, be avoided at all costs if the process of *da'wah* is to be set in motion and continue in an atmosphere of freedom.

The Prophet Muhammad ﷺ foresaw that religious coercion would not be used as a weapon by secular rulers. His insight told him that in future in the secular sphere the principle of religious freedom would become so established and thoroughly consolidated that no secular ruler would ever attempt to put a curb on religious freedom. And that if this problem ever arose, it would be due to the adoption of some wrong policy, or the committing of some blunder by the believers themselves. That is why the Prophet gave extremely important guidelines as an advance warning to Muslims.

In books of *hadith*, there are a large number of traditions which foretell the setting in of corruption in the Muslim rulers of later times, yet Muslims were strictly forbidden to wage war on them in the name of political reform. The Muslims were rather enjoined to keep their distance from them, to take to the hills (that is, to stay away from political activities) and to devote themselves to tending their sheep and goats. That is to say that they had to abandon the path of political confrontation in favour of continuing their activities in non-political fields, such as education, *da'wah*, the service of the Qur'an and *hadith*, etc.

In the first phase of Islam, it was Abdullah ibn Zubayr who violated this prohibition. He engaged in an armed confrontation with the Umayyad ruler, Yazid ibn Muawaiya, in the name of reform in politics. It resulted in the loss of precious Muslim lives and resources. At that time, Abdullah ibn Umar, son of the second caliph and companion of the Prophet, was in Makkah, yet he did not take part in the fighting. Some companions of Abdullah ibn Zubayr met him and asked him to join in the battle. The conversation that took place on this occasion has been recorded in *Sahih al-Bukhari* under three references.

One account has been thus recorded: Nafe narrates that during the (*fitna*) revolt by Ibn Zubayr, two persons came and said to Ibn Umar that people were being killed, while he, the son of Umar (the second caliph) as well as a senior companion of the Prophet, refused to take part in the campaign. They asked him what prevented him from doing so. He replied: "I refrain from joining in this battle because of God's express command never to shed the blood of one's brother: it is unlawful." Both replied: "Has not God enjoined us to fight till persecution (fitna) ceases?" Abdullah ibn Umar then retorted: "We fought till *fitna* ceased. Religion became only for God, and now you want to fight so that fitna may return, and religion will no longer be for God." (*Fathul Bari*, *Kitab at-Tafsir*, vol. 8, p.32, *Kitab al-Fitan* Vol. 13, p. 49).

From this account we learn that war against persecution as commanded by God was limited in its scope and of a particular nature. It had to be directed against those leaders who had established a system of religious persecution; who were not ready to grant to believers in monotheism the liberty to practise their faith. The companions of the Prophet waged war against such oppression, first of all in Arabia, and then in major parts of Asia and Africa, and succeeded in bringing it to an end. Thenceforth, believers in Islam had full freedom to practise their religion and to invite others to answer its call.

After the successful conclusion of this movement against religious coercion, the believers began living in an atmosphere of religious freedom. But during the reign of the Umayyads, when the rot of corruption had begun to set in, certain Muslims, referring to this verse of the Qur'an, engaged themselves in armed conflict with the rulers. To all intents and purposes, the battle was for a good cause: they wanted to oust these corrupt caliphs and replace them with men who were virtuous and just. But, in reality, their actions proved counter-productive.

The Prophet Muhammad ﷺ foresaw that the effort at political reform would, in effect, culminate in nothing but destruction. It would only replace a lesser evil with a greater evil. That is why he had issued a stern, prior warning, expressly commanding his people to confine their activities to non-political fields and to opt for a policy of avoidance as regards corruption in political institutions.

In books of *hadith* a number of traditions have been recorded on this subject under the heading of *fitna*. It was thanks to these traditions that, after the development of the Islamic sciences (in terms of which commentaries on the traditions were written), religious scholars arrived at a consensus that it was totally unlawful to revolt against an established Muslim government, regardless of how justified such action might appear to be.

The famous traditionist, Imam al-Nawawi, has commented on the tradition regarding fitna as recorded in *Sahih Muslim*:

> These traditions clearly convey that we should not enter into any confrontation with political rulers. Even if we find in them any major deviation from Islam, our responsibility will be limited purely to the giving of advice in private. According to the consensus of Muslim scholars, so far as revolt and armed confrontation are concerned, even if the rulers in question are corrupt and tyrannical these actions are unlawful (haraam). (*Sahih Muslim*, with the commentary of an-Nawawi, *Kitab al-Imarah*, vol. 12, p.229).

From this commentary, we learn that the waging of war against fitna in no way meant the replacing of non-Muslim governments with Muslim regimes. Its actual purpose was to put an end to the use of intellectual and ideological coercion, so that God's servants might be at liberty to perform their devotions to God and communicate God's message in an atmosphere of freedom. Waging war against Muslim rulers will certainly result in a revival of the coercive system, for the rulers will not hesitate to resort to oppression in order to keep their political power intact. The upshot will be that the old *fitna* will re-emerge in a new garb. That is why the Prophet Muhammad œ strictly forbade such action and Islamic scholars arrived at a consensus that according to the Islamic shariah, insurrection against an established Muslim government was unlawful. Even in unavoidable situations, Muslims are required to strive peacefully and to refrain entirely from launching violent movements aimed at unseating those in positions of authority.

This is undoubtedly an important Islamic injunction. It has great wisdom behind it. To put it briefly, the kings of ancient times made every effort to politicize religion. And when they found the adherents of any given religion placing obstacles in their path, they went all out to crush them. In a similar way, even today, certain factions attempt to Islamize governments, then those rulers who become their targets, wreak all kinds of havoc on Islamists in order to save their political power.

The solution to this problem, as laid down in Islam, is to refrain from setting oneself on a collision course with the rulers. If any evil is found in them, the course to adopt is to give advice, privately, at the individual level, and to avoid all public condemnation or armed clashes. This sage counsel was given by Islam, so that the basic task of propagating and consolidating the religion might continue unhampered in non-political fields.

The manner of working of the traditionists gives us a good historical example. The gigantic task of the compilation of the traditions in the first phase of Islam lasted from the time of the Umayyad empire till that of the Abbasid empire. Without doubt, the rot had set in in the Muslim rulers. But the Islamic scholars of this period did not launch any movement against them. Remaining aloof from politics, they continued to serve the cause of the *hadith*. It is the result of this wise policy on their part that today we possess in compiled form the precious treasure of the Prophet's traditions. If the traditions of those days had opted to set themselves up against these Muslim rulers, they would have met the same fate as that of Abdullah ibn Zubayr, Husain ibn Ali, Nafs Zakiyya, etc. any political *jihad* engaged in by these traditionists would have come to the same disastrous end. All the people concerned would have been assassinated by the rulers, — as had happened with other political opponents. And then the inestimable wealth of the traditions would have been buried along with the traditionists, in whose memories they had been preserved.

From a study of the Qur'an and *hadith*, we find that the actual target of a religious mission is the Islamization of the individual rather than the State. The domination of Islam at the level of the state is only an offshoot of the religious mission and not its actual target.

The Qur'an has clearly stated that, for believers, political power is a gift from God, and not a goal to be striven for. That is why the Qur'an observes:

> God has promised those of you who believe and do good works to make them masters in the land as He had made their ancestors before them, to strengthen the faith he chose for them and to change their fears to safety. Let them worship me and serve no other gods besides me. Wicked indeed are they who after this deny Me (24:55).

The same point has been made in a tradition of the Prophet: Just as you will be, so will be your rulers. (*Mishkat al-Masabih*).

In actual fact this tradition tells us of a law of nature. The political power of a country depends upon its people. Any system which has the acceptance of the public will perpetuate itself, while a system which is anathema to the people will prove unsustainable. In a truly Islamic society, an un-Islamic political regime cannot take root, and cannot therefore be self-perpetuating. That is why Islam has enjoined the targeting of individuals for Islamic reform. If in any society a large number of people follow Islam, both in the letter and in the spirit, such a society will on its own come under the direction of political power based on Islam.

This separation of *da'wah* activism and political confrontation was crucial. It was by virtue of this separation that the propagation of Islam continued unhampered for a period of a thousand years after the emergence of Islam, until the number of Muslims rose to one billion. Without this, the great achievement of the dissemination of Islam could never have become a reality.

The wisdom of this teaching of Islam has become clearer than ever today. In present times two revolutions have taken place contemporaneously. After a long historical process, religious freedom has been held to be an irrevocable right of human beings all over the world. Today, the right to believe and practive and propagate any religion of one's choice has become an established right of human beings. This freedom has only one condition: that in the availing of these rights, one should not engage in violence of any sort. The adoption of violence will render the practice and propagation of one's religion impossible, whatever the part of the world that might be.

Another great revolution of our times has come in the form of modern communications, which has rendered the spread of Islam much more effective than hitherto. The print and electronic media, as well as other means of communication, have opened all the doors to the global dissemination of the message of Islam. Now the task of *da'wah* in the present age has been so greatly facilitated that it seems as rapid and easy as the diffusion of the sun's rays across the earth.

The Peaceful Propagation of Islam

Referring to Christ and his followers, the Qur'an tells us:

When Isa (Christ) observed their refusal he asked:

Who will be my supporters in the cause of God?
The disciples replied: We are the supporters of
God. We believe in Him. Bear witness that we have
surrendered ourselves to Him. (3:52)

The response given by the disciples to the call of Jesus was so appropriate that the same response was likewise demanded by the Muslims. Therefore the Qur'an says:

O Believers, be God's helpers. When Christ the son
of Mary said to the disciples, 'Who will come with
me to the help of God?' They replied: 'We are
God's helpers.' Some of the children of Israel
believed in Him, while others did not. We aided
the believers against their enemies and they
triumphed over them. (61:14)

On deeper reflection we find that this verse is of relevance to the history of the second stage of Islam, that is, the second period of the Muslim *ummah* (community). That was when *fitna* had ceased and religious freedom had been introduced into the world. Then the Muslims had to adopt the same course as that adopted by the followers of Christ under his guidance. Of course, there was no question of adopting the additions and innovations in their religious beliefs; these were to be rejected. Therefore, leaving aside the system of their beliefs, the practical pattern adopted by them in *da'wah* was without doubt a prophetic pattern. And it was as worth adopting for the Muslims as it was for the Christians.

The question arises as to what kind of "help" Christ had asked his followers to give. We find the answer in the traditions. Ibn Hisham, the Prophet's biographer of the first phase, writes: "I have received it from reliable sources that Abu Bakr al-Huzali narrated that, one day, after the peace treaty of Hudaibiya, the Prophet came to his companions and said, 'O people, God has sent me as a mercy to all the nations of the world, therefore, do not differ as the disciples of Christ differed with Christ.' The Prophet's companions asked: 'O Messenger of God, how did the disciples of Christ differ from their Prophet?' The Prophet replied: 'Christ invited the disciples to what I have invited you. So those who were sent to nearby places, happily accepted it, but those who were sent to distant places were reluctant to go. Then Christ complained to God about it, so God's special succour descended upon them and these disciples began speaking the language of the community to which they were being sent."(*Seerat an-Nabi*, Ibn Hisham, vol. 4/279).

This incident has been recorded in the present Bible. Here are some exerpts in brief:

> Go ye therefore and make disciples of all the nations. (Matthew, 28:19).

> And the gospel must first be preached among all the nations. (Mark, 13:10).

> Go ye into all the world and preach the gospel to every creature. (Mark, 16:15).

In obedience to these injunctions of Christ, his followers left Palestine. After Christ had left the world, they spread over different cities and countries. They propagated their religion peacefully and those who embraced their faith also adopted the path of peace in propagating the divine message. In this way, the spread of Christianity continued from generation to generation.

As a result of this non-aggressive activity on the part of the followers of Christ, within a period of two hundred years after the advent of Christianity, it spread to many eastern countries. Subsequently, these Christians entered Europe. Here they were initially faced with great difficulties. However, they quietly began propagating Christianity until the time came when the European Emperor Constantine the Great came under its influence, converted to Christianity in 337 and proclaimed it to be the official religion of his empire. Subsequently, the majority of Europeans entered the Christian fold.

The Qur'an tells us that during the life of Christ, God decreed that the followers of Christ should prevail over their enemies.

In the third chapter of the Qur'an, addressing Christ, God said: "I shall.... Exalt your followers above them (the disbelievers) till the Day of Resurrection." (3:55). Similarly, in chapter 61, the Qur'an has this to say:

> We aided the believers (in Christ) against their
> enemies, and they triumphed over them. (61:14).

Here the question arises as to how the followers of Christ came to dominate them. Surely this did not come about as a result of war and violence. For neither by the Qur'an, nor by historical records can it be established that the Christians engaged in armed confrontations with their religious opponents.

According to historical records, the number of Christ's followers continued increasing until a time came when, by the sheer ratio of their numbers, they came to enjoy a position of dominance. This leads us to ask what feature of the propagation of their mission was so especially effective as to cause their numbers to increase so rapidly. The Qur'an states that this came about with the special succour of God: "We gave Christ the gospel and put compassion and mercy in the hearts of his followers." (57:27) We find the same sentiments expressed in the Bible in the words uttered by Christ:

> But I say to you who hear: love your enemies, do good to those who hate you, bless those who curse you, and pray for those who spitefully use you. To him who strikes you on the one cheek, offer the other also. And from him who takes away your cloak, do not withhold your tunic either. Give to everyone who asks of you. And from him who takes away your goods, do not ask them back. And just as you want men to do to you, also do to them likewise. But if you love those who love you, what credit is that to you? For even sinners love those who love them. And if you do good to those who do good to you, what credit is that to you? For even sinners do the same. And if you lend to those from whom you hope to receive back, what credit is that to you? For even sinners lend to sinners to receive as much back. But love your enemies, do good, and lend, hoping for nothing in return; and your reward will be great, and you will be sons of the Most High. For He is kind to the unthankful and evil. Therefore be merciful, just as your Father

also is merciful. Judge not, and you shall not be judged. Condemn not, and you shall not be condemned. Forgive, and you will be forgiven. Give and it will be given to you: good measure, pressed down, shaken together, and running over will be put into your bosom. For with the same measure that you use, it will be measured back to you. (Luke 6:27-38)

This untterance of Christ indicates what kind of character a man with a mission should have. Normal human relations between the *da'i* and the *madu'* (the person addressed) are essential for the success of any *da'wah* mission. The only way to establish a favourable atmosphere is for the *da'i* to adopt the ethics of unilateralism, that is to behave well, consistently and unconditionally, even if his hearers (the *madu'*) do not behave well towards him. In refusing to copy the attitude and conduct of the *madu'*, the *da'i* adheres to the highest code of ethics based on Islamic principles.

"And from him who takes away your cloak, do not withhold your tunic either." (Luke, 6:29) We are told here in symbolic language what our behaviour should be. The *da'i* does all he can so that no controversy is created between himself and the madu; all he does is convey the message of *da'wah*. That is why the *da'i* takes sole responsibility for the maintaining of a propitious atmosphere for *da'wah* by unilaterally bringing all controversies to an end. Such an approach was not peculiar to Christianity; it was a feature common to the missions of all of the prophets. This principle of unilateral accommodation is a sine qua non for success in the task of *da'wah*.

The followers of Christ wholeheartedly adopted this

teaching of their Prophet. This special feature of their missionary character contributed extraordinarily to the spread of the Christian religion. They made such headway, that they gave new meaning to the principle of peaceful proselytism. And then, along with their teaching, they engaged in such social service as proved an effective means of bringing the *madu'* closer to them. It was the result of this particular *da'wah* style that Christianity spread all over, becoming the greatest world religion.

There is a tradition recorded in *Sahih Muslim* which foretells us this rapid spread of the Christian religion:

> Mustaurid Qarashi related that he heard the Prophet say that Doomsday would not come until the Christians were the greatest in number. When these words of the Prophet were conveyed to Amr ibn al-As (a senior companion of the Prophet and the conqueror and governor of Egypt) he asked Mustaurid: 'What is the nature of these traditions you are narrating?' Mustaurid replied: 'I narrate only what I have heard from the Prophet.' Amr ibn al-As said: 'If you say so (that is, if it is an authentic *hadith*) then the Christians are undoubtedly the most forbearing in times of adversity, take no time in setting themselves in order after a calamity and are better than others in caring for their weak and deprived.' (*Sahih Muslim, Kitab al-Fitan*).

From these details we find that a major aim of the revolution brought about by the Prophet and his companions was to remove all obstacles in the path of *da'wah*, so that such conducive conditions would prevail as would encourage people to practice God's religion and invite others to the same path. This process had to be continued from generation to generation.

The first stage of this revolution was marked by the coercive system being brought to an end, ushering in the dawn of religious freedom in the world. The second stage was embarked upon, when, by availing of the advantages of this freedom, Muslims disseminated Islam at the universal level. Now the Muslims are in the third and final stage of their history, when the progress of religious freedom has reached its zenith. Now Muslims have to continue the task of conveying the truth to people and it is imperative that they do so by adherence to peaceful methods. The truly shining example of religious achievement, according to the testimony of the Qur'an, is that of the followers of Christ.

Judging by the above-quoted words of Abdullah ibn Umar, the obstacles in the path of *da'wah* work have been removed forever. If obstacles reappear, this will surely be as a result of some ill-considered policy pursued by the Muslims themselves. If the Muslims are able to refrain from adopting any erroneous course, no real obstacle should ever come in the way of the call of the truth until the advent of Doomsday.

22

❧❧❧

The Role of Non-Muslims
in Islamic Development

Islam is the religion of Nature, and in treading its path,
it is non-discriminatory, finding room within its scheme
of things for every segment of society. Rigidity is quite
alien to its process of development.

There is a meaningful *hadith* in *Sahih al-Bukhari* to this
effect. According to this *hadith*, the Prophet Muhammad ﷺ
said: "God Almighty will strengthen this religion [Islam]
through a *fajir* (one who is not a true Muslim) person as well
(Bukhari).

This is a very important declaration because in this
world, any natural process begins with the involvement of
different elements—as happened in the case of Islam.
Humanity as a whole is an interdependent body and Islam
is not an exception.

Islam is an ideology aimed at human development,
and no process of human development can endure without
involving humanity at large. There are several phases in
the history of Islam which illustrate this point.

The Prophet Muhammad ﷺ spent his first thirteen years of prophethood in Makkah. At that time in Makkah, there existed a tribal system. There was no organized state in the modern sense. It was necessary for everyone to have protection under one of the tribal chiefs. So, according to this prevalent custom, the Prophet availed himself of the protection of two of the local chieftains—Abu Talib and Mut'im bin Adi alternatively, both of whom happened to be non-Muslims.

After spending thirteen years in Makkah, the Prophet migrated to Madinah. It was a very risky journey because his opponents had announced a reward of a hundred camels to anyone who would bring them the Prophet's head. In spite of this, the Prophet chose a member of the rival group to be his guide for the journey, because this guide was known to be an honest person in his profession. He is known in Islamic history as Abdullah bin Urayqit. He was a non-Muslim and died as a non-Muslim in Makkah.

After the migration of the Prophet, a series of armed conflicts broke out between the Prophet and his opponents. One of the military campaigns of his opponents, known in Islamic history as Ghazwa al-Ahzab, was so devastating that even the Qur'an refers to it as one of the most terrifying moments in Islamic history. At the time, the Muslims had become quite helpless against their opponents. The only thing that eased this most difficult of situations was the role a Madinite played—that of a middleman.

This man came to the Prophet in the night when Madinah was surrounded by enemy forces. He said, "I have become a Muslim in my heart, but I have not made it public yet. So the mushriks and the Jews both have trust in me." Realizing that this man was in a position to play a peace-making role between the two parties, since he was trusted by both, the Prophet said, "You are the only one in this position among us."

This man began, therefore, to negotiate between the two parties and history tells us that it was he who cleared the path to peace at this juncture between the two rival parties. It was because of his efforts that the enemy decided to lift the siege of the city of Madinah and return to their homes.

Islamic history contains many examples of the role played by non-Muslims in the development of Islam. This principle of non-Muslim involvement in Islamic development can also be extended from an individual level to the level of an entire group.

In the present day context, Western Civilization is an appropriate example. Although Western Civilization developed in non-Muslim societies without any direct contribution from the Muslim minds, it is helpful for Islam in many aspects. For example, it is this Western Civilization that finally ended religious persecution and opened the door for religious freedom and da'wah. Similarly, it is this Western Civilization which has developed the modern means of communication that has made it possible for Muslims to do da'wah work on a global scale. Also, modern scientific discoveries made in the West have paved the way to proving the beliefs of Islam on a scientific basis.

In previous times, it was assumed that the truths of Islam, or religion for that matter, could be supported only by arguments that were inferential in nature and not by arguments that were direct. But modern science, in bringing human thought from a macrocosmic level to a microcosmic level, has made it possible to accept that inferential reasoning is as valid as direct reasoning. This development has allowed Islam to prove its truth on the same level as scientific theories are proven.

From these few examples, it is clear that non-Muslims are also helpful to the cause of Islam in many ways. Islamic development is such a universal process that all Muslim and non-Muslim forces contribute towards its fulfillment.

This aspect of a role for those other than Muslims in the development of Islam serves a moral end as well. It makes Muslims sympathetic towards the rest of the world so that the hearts of Muslims are filled with love for others instead of hate, enmity and distrust.

The contribution of non-Muslims to Islam has not been of a temporary nature. It has continued throughout Islamic history. In present times these contributions made by non-Muslims, especially in the field of scientific discoveries, have been far greater than ever before.

What are these scientific discoveries? They are, in actual fact, the discoveries of nature. Nature, or in the words of the Qur'an, "all the things of the heavens and the earth" are signs of God. Accordingly, all the things of the universe serve as scientific argument for Islamic teachings. In this respect the discoveries of nature are in fact the discoveries of the divine realities which testify to the truth of the teachings of Islam. I have gone into considerable detail on this point in other books. Here I wish to give only one example to illustrate my point.

There is a verse in the Qur'an:

> We shall save your body this day, so that you may
> be a sign for those who come after you. (10:92)

This refers to the Egyptian ruler, Pharoah, a contemporary of the Prophet Moses. As we know, Pharoah had been drowned by God in the deep waters of the sea. At that moment God had decreed the preservation of Pharaoh's body in order that it might be a sign of God for future generations.

However, neither at the time of revelation of the Qur'an, nor even a thousand years later, did anyone have had any knowledge regarding Pharaoh's body; it remained absolutely unknown to the Muslim world. It was not until the end of the nineteenth century that this preserved body was discovered. This prediction of the Qur'an had been fulfilled to the letter. However, this task was performed entirely by non-Muslims.

It was a French scholar, Prof. Loret, who discovered this mummified body of Pharoah at Thebes in the King's Valley, from where it was transported to Cairo. Prof. Elliot Smith removed its wrapping on the 8th of July, 1907. He gives a detailed description of this operation and examination of the body in his book, *The Royal Mummies* (1912).

In June 1975, Dr. Maurice Bucaille was allowed by the Egyptian authorities to examine Pharoah's body. Special investigations were made during this examination of this mummified body along with a team of specialists. By means of several modern techniques like radiography, Carbon-dating, and endoscopy, the exact period of this body was established. After study and research lasting several years by a team of western experts, it was scientifically proved that this body definitely belonged exactly to the period of Moses.

It was also established beyond any doubt that this Pharoah died either from drowning or from very violent shocks preceding the moment when he was drowned.

The French author, Dr Maurice Bucaille, rounds off the chapter called 'The Exodus' in his book, *The Bible, the Qur'an and Science*, with these thrilling words:

> Those who seek among modern data for proof of the veracity of the Holy scriptures will find a magnificent illustration of the verses of the Qur'an dealing with the Pharoah's body by visiting the Royal Mummies' Room of the Egyptian Museum, Cairo. (p 241).

23

❀ᘎ❀

Conversion: An Intellectual
Transformation

When an individual belonging to one religious group
joins another religious group after converting to that
religion, that, in religious terminology, is called proselytism.
But this is a limited concept of conversion, which needs to
be viewed in a more scientific light.

The religious view of conversion relates only to
religious tradition. In this respect it is relatively limited in
its spectrum. The scientific outlook, on the contrary, is
much broader in scope, being based on the eternal principles
of nature itself. Although it would be proper to say that,
in the religious context conversion for human beings is a
matter of choice, in the scientific sense, this is not so. It is
an eternal principle of life, in exactly the same way as the
laws of nature have the status of being immutable. We are
compelled to accept the principle of conversion, just as we
are compelled to accept the morning following the evening,
or one season coming after another.

Islam and Conversion

Conversion in Islamic thought is not synonymous with proselytism in the formal sense. It is an event which takes place in a person's life as a result of intellectual revolution or spiritual transformation. It is not simply leaving one religious tradition for another. The Islamic ideal of conversion is for the individual to discover the truth after an exhaustive search for it and then by his own choice, abandon one religion for another.

During his final phase in 6 AH, the Prophet Muhammad ﷺ sent letters to the neighbouring rulers of his time, by which they were directly invited to accept the message of Islam. For instance, in his letter to the Byzantine Emperor Heraclius I, the Prophet wrote these words: "Accept Islam and you will be blessed with peace." Similarly at any gatherings which took place in Makkah the Prophet would make a point of going to that place and address the assembled people thus: "O people, say there is no god but God and you will attain God's grace."

At first glance this was an invitation to people to change their religion. But the study of the Qur'an tells us that it was in actual fact an invitation to a transformation in thinking, and not a change of religion in the simple sense. In the first phase of Islam, some Arab Bedouins had accepted Islam just by reciting the *kalima*, the creed of Islam, while they had not undergone any change in character at a deeper level. The Qur'an admonished them in strong terms:

> The Arabs of the desert say 'We believe.' Say. "You have not believed yet; but rather say, 'We have accepted Islam, for the true faith has not yet entered into your hearts.'" (49:14).

From this we learn that conversion according to Islam means a thorough transformation of the person and not just a change of religion in the everyday sense.

There is a formal method of religious conversion prevalent among the Jews and Christians known as baptism. In this ritual ceremony the convert is dipped in water. The hue of water considered a symbol of purity, and their priests believe that dipping someone in pure clean water purifies him, and he is thus converted to a new religion. But pouring water outwardly does not purify a person, for the attainment of purity necessitates a transformation of the total human personality. The convert is suffused with the hue of God and he adopts God's ways in thought, word and deed.

As the Qur'an puts it:

> We take on God's own dye—and who has a better dye than God's? And we are His worshippers. (2:138).

The Qur'an refuses to give its seal of approval to conversions which are mere formalities. In ancient Madinah there was the case of about three hundred people having become Muslims by reciting the Islamic creed. To all intents and purposes they even said their prayers, and fasted, but they did all this in a hypocritical manner, paying only lip service: their inner state did not correspond to their outward pronouncements. They claimed allegiance to Islam by word of mouth but, as regards the state of their hearts, the Islamic spirit was lacking. The Qur'an branded the 'Islam' of such people as a falsity:

When the hypocrites come to you, they say:

'We bear witness that you are God's apostle.' God
knows that you are indeed His Messenger, and
God bears witness that the hypocrites are lying.
(63:1)

What is meant by true religious conversion is illustrated
by an incident in which some verses from the Qur'an were
read to a gathering of Christians. About seventy of them
were so deeply moved that they abandoned their ancestral
religion and converted to Islam. As the Qur'an puts it:
When they listen to that which was revealed to the
Messenger, you will see their eyes filled with tears as they
recognize its truth. They say: 'Lord, we believe. Count us
among Your witnesses. Why should we not believe in God
and in the truth that has come down to us? Why should we
not hope for admission among the righteous?' (5:83-84)

Similarly, the Qur'an speaks of true believers "as those
whose hearts are filled with awe at the mention of God, and
whose faith grows stronger as they listen to His revelations.
They are those who put their trust in their Lord, pray
steadfastly, and spend of that which We have given them.
Such are the true believers. They shall have degrees with
their Lord and shall be forgiven by Him, and a generous
provision shall be made for them. (6:2-4)

This shows that religious conversion in actual fact is
the result of a realization. When the individual's search for
truth finds a convincing answer, this is such a profound
experience that his heart is intensely moved. His eyes are
filled with tears. His whole existence is moulded in the cast
of truth. It is then that he emerges a new and altogether
different person, having undergone a transformation.

That is why the Qur'an uses no synonym for conversion.

To express the act of conversion, other more meaningful words have been used, for instance, the *da'wah* mission (the communication of the message to others) of Islam finds mention in the Qur'an in these words:

> A light has come to you from God and a glorious Book with which He will guide to the paths of peace those that seek to please Him. He will lead them by His will from darkness to the light; He will guide them to a straight path. (5:15-16)

Those who enter the fold of Islam after being influenced by their study of the Qur'an, have been thus described in the Qur'an:

> Is then he who knows that what has been revealed to you by your Lord is the truth, like him who is blind? Truly, none will take heed but the wise. (13:19)

According to this verse, the real conversion is one which has taken place when the convert is aware that he has entered the phase of gnosis and has left behind the phase of ignorance. That is why a tradition of the Prophet speaks of the period prior to Islam as a period of ignorance.

Similarly, the difference between a believer and a non-believer has been alluded to in the Qur'an in the context of life after death: 'Can the dead man whom We have raised to life and given a light with which he may be guided among men, be compared to him who blunders about in a darkness from which he will never emerge?' (6:123)

This same reality has been expressed in different ways in the Qur'an, for instance, by the simile of the earth. When the rains come, the fertile earth blooms, becoming green with vegetation. 'Good soil yields fruit by God's leave. But poor and scant are the fruits which spring from barren soil. Thus we show our signs to those who render thanks.' (7:58)

Then there is the parable of the tree:

> Do you not see how God compares a good word to a good tree whose root is firm with its branches in the sky, yielding its fruit every season by God's leave? God gives parables to men so that they may become mindful. But an evil word is like an evil tree torn out of the earth, and has no stability. God will strengthen the faithful with His steadfast word, both in this life and in the Hereafter. He leaves the wrongdoers in error. God accomplishes what He pleases. (14:24-27)

These verses from the Qur'an tell us the difference between one who has found the truth and one who has failed to do so. The latter is like the shrub growing on the upper surface of the soil: it is short-lived, either vanishing on its own or being pulled out, and is of no use to mankind. The former resembles a profitable, fruitful tree putting its roots deep down into the earth. It seems that it is for the earth and the earth is for it. Receiving sustenance from the earth as well as the atmosphere, it benefits people in many ways. Rooted as it is in the earth, it has a desirable and meaningful existence.

Conversion a universal principle

Another aspect of conversion, pointed out repeatedly in the Qur'an, is that it is not confined solely to religion. It is rather a universal principle, by which all kinds of progress have been set in motion. The present universe was originally composed of condensed matter, then it underwent a process of internal change, by which it began expanding until this vast universe, with which we are now familiar, was formed. (21:30). Similarly, the earth lies dry and barren, then it is transformed by the rain so that, "it begins to stir and swell, putting forth every kind of radiant bloom." (22:5)

Again, some apparently unformed matter passes through well-defined stages in the womb, until it assumes the form of a complete living creature—this goes for both humans as well as animals. Then grass and grains enter the cow's belly and, by a certain natural system undergo a transformation, until grass and grains are converted into milk, a very precious food for man (16:66).

By citing such natural phenomena, the Qur'an demonstrates how this world has been established on the universal principle of conversion. Here all kinds of progress are instigated through the process of transformation. For instance, the combination of two gases resulting in water, iron being transformed into steel, chemical combinations of various kinds producing useful metals, etc.

All these are examples of conversion in its broader sense. The same kind of conversion is at work in the world of human thought. There is an ongoing interchange of ideas in this world. Through this process one school of thought gives way to another, better school of thought. For instance, for several hundred years the geo-centric theory of the solar system dominated world thought. Then as a result of intellectual advances it began to erode, until finally it was rejected by the academic world, being replaced by the helio-centric theory, this having stood the test of observation. Conversion in the world of thought is called religious conversion, which is only a small part of the vaster scheme of nature.

The truth is that conversion is a universal law established by nature itself, on the basis of which all the material progress of the modern world has been taking place. Just as the physical growth of living beings (humans and animals) has depended wholly on this principle of conversion, so also has all the progress made in the world of thought over thousands of years. That is, theories have become established truths when proven by available facts. In this world no meaningful development can take shape without going through this process of conversion. This is especially true of the acceptance of religion, which is another name for recognition of spiritual truth. Only that religion can become one's own which has been discovered as a result of personal struggle. Religion is deeply related to conviction and conviction in turn is related to discovery. There is no conviction without discovery and there is no religion without conviction.

The true follower of a religion is not one who is simply born into it. Finding religion must be a matter of conviction and is possible only after a long period of self-analysis. Then the would-be adherent should feel that he is rediscovering something of which he is already in possession.

The reality of Conversion

Conversion does not mean just saying some formal words, changing one's name and leaving one cultural group to join another. It entails not just an outward change of religion, but a profound alteration of the mindset after passing through many stages of soul-searching and self-analysis. Conversion, in essence, is the emergence of a new individual—one of the most significant events of human history, for it is only with the proliferation of such spiritually reformed personalities that any given society will attain true moral uplift, and reach the highest levels of achievement.

Conversion, in reality, is an event resulting from a sense of discovery. After making a great discovery, one does not remain as before. One becomes a new man. Only a truly revolutionary change of this kind merits the name of conversion. When it does take place, it stems from personal decision-making, and not from greed or external pressures. It causes those lacking in awareness to become intellectually receptive; the dormant come fully alive in all their senses; the morally "blind" gain a code of ethics; the incurious develop a questing spirit; those living in a circumscribed environment suddenly enter a world without limits, where they can breathe freely; creatures existing at the purely physical level rise above it and begin really to live on a higher conceptual plane; the aimless wanderer, becoming spiritually focussed, learns the secret of leading a purposeful life.

Conversion—A Healthy Historical Process

A few years ago I went through a book by an Indian writer called *The Politics of Conversion*. I found that there was only one point on which I differed from the author and that was the choice of title for the book. I felt that it might more justifiably have been called *The Politicisation of Conversion*. This would have underscored the necessity to avoid the sensationalism of giving a political hue to something which was, after all, a natural reality.

What is conversion? Usually conversion is equated with proselytism. But conversion, in its broadest sense, is much further-reaching, in that it is a universal principle of nature. It is a historical process—healthy and inexorable—and attempting to put a stop to it would be like trying to put a stop to history itself. And who in this world has the power to do so? Conversion, in reality, is the birth of an entirely new entity resulting from the encounter between old and new schools of thought. This is a universal law established by nature itself.

The study of human history reveals that a certain process is always at work, which Carl Marx had wrongly called dialectical materialism. More rightly this is a dialogue-conversion process. That is, when two systems of thought clash with each other, an intellectual revolution ensues.

This dialogue-conversion process is the only ladder to all kinds of human progress. That is, whenever any revolution of civilization has been produced or a human group has succeeded in performing some great creative role, it has always come in the wake of this same dialogue-conversion process.

There is no single form of this process. It can be religious or non-religious in nature. In the history of the last fifteen hundred years we find two major examples—one of religious conversion and the other of secular conversion.

The history of the Arabs provides the example of religious conversion. Up to the sixth century A.D., the Arabs led a confined tribal life under the idolatrous system.

Then at the beginning of the seventh century, there appeared the religion of monotheism, Islam. In consequence, intensive dialogue began between the monotheists and idolators. This dialogue assumed such an aggressive character that it came to the point of collision. As a result a new way of thinking was born among the Arabs, which went on growing till it took the form of a great intellectual revolution.

This intellectual revolution, or this discovery of a new idea, resulted in the emergence of a new personality among the Arabs. In the words of a European historian, every one of them acquired such a revolutionary personality that their entire people became a nation of heroes. Within just fifty years they brought about that historical event which is called by a historian "the miracle of all miracles." Briffault puts this in a nutshell: "But for the Arabs, western civilization would never have arisen at all."

Another example is that of the European Christian nations. After the crusades—a historical process extending over several hundred years—these nations too went through a conversion process. This conversion was secular rather than religious. Intense conflict took place between science and religion. This is elucidated in the book: *Conflict Between Science and Religion*."

This encounter continued for several hundred years in the form of dialogue and conflict, until a new intellectual revolution was produced within the European nations and they finally bade good-bye to the old and opted for the new. This revolution is known as the Renaissance.

It was this revolution which enabled the European nations to perform the greatest feat of history, i.e. emerging from the traditional age into the age of science. The truth is that the human mind is a treasure-house of unlimited power. In normal situations the human brain remains in a dormant state. It is only external shocks which awaken it, and the greater they are the greater the intellectual revolution within man. This shock treatment produces in man what psychologists call brain storming. This brings about a fresh intellectual outlook, a transformation which elevates a normal man to the level of a superman, who is then able to perform great feats.

Religious conversion is only a small part of this whole process. When the dialogue-conversion process is set in motion, it cannot have limits set to it. It is not possible to allow one kind of conversion and to prohibit another. Being a stormy process, it is boundless.

It must be appreciated that there are two major kinds of religious conversion—inner faith conversion and inter faith conversion. Now let us take an example of inter faith conversion. There was a multi-lingual Bengali Doctor of Philosophy, Nishi Kant Chattopadhyaye, who, having first studied philosophy, then all major religions, faced intellectual confrontation with different faiths. Finally he made an intellectual discovery in consequence of which he left his ancestral religion, Hinduism, in favour of Islam. His Muslim name was Azizuddin. He delivered a lecture, published later under the title, *Why I Have Embraced Islam*, which describes in detail the story of his intellectual development. This lecture has been reproduced in one of the chapters of this book.

There have also been instances of men and women who were born in Muslim families, who later cast off their family religion in order to turn into secularists, or even atheists in some cases. However, sooner or later they reached a turning point in their lives when they came back to Islam as sincere practising Muslims.

The author of this book is an example of this kind of inner faith conversion. He was born in a Muslim family and until 1942, kept on performing all religious duties and rituals under the influence of the family. Then, an intellectual revolt took place in his mind against Islam and consequently he became a totally irreligious person for many years to come. It was not until 1948, after five years of systematic analytical study of modern philosophy, science and religion, that the author was fully convinced of the continuing relevance and credibility of Islam and decided to return to it again. But, this time it was a return, or conversion, to a consciously chosen and rediscovered Islam, not to the traditionally inherited one.

To sum up, conversion is a universal and inescapable law of nature. A study of psychology and history tells us that, in order to give a new impetus to an individual or a group and to bring about a moral and intellectual revolution, what is most effective is the sense of discovery. This feeling of having discovered some truth which was as yet unknown, awakens all the dormant powers of the individual. This feeling turns an ordinary man into a superman. It is such supermen who cross the ocean, who scale mountains, and who by their heroic character cause history to enter a new age. Today, human history is once again facing a deadlock. History is once again in need of people who pass through this experience of a discovery. For it is such people, charged with new spiritual power, who will give a strong push to human history to enter a new and a better age.

24

❧✿❧

*A Case of Discovery**

I t is a trite saying, that the present can be fully grasped and appreciated only by a due reference to the past. In order, therefore, to set before you clearly the reasons that have induced me to accept Islam in preference to the other great religions of the world, it is necessary that I should

---

* This chapter is a lecture which was delivered by Dr. Nishikant Chattopadhyaye in 1904, in Hyderabad. He belonged to a well-known Bengali family, which earned much fame and popularity as one of its family members, Sarojini Naidu, daughter of Agornath Chattopadhyaye, played an eminent role in the freedom struggle. Dr. Nishikant was a close relative of Mr Naidu.

This family migrated from Bengal to settle in Hyderabad during the British Period. One of its learned members was Dr. Nishikant Chattopadhyaye, who also made this migratory journey. Well versed in several languages, he was a true seeker in the real sense of the word. He studied religion and its related disciplines in detail. Finally he became fully convinced of the veracity of Islam. Having found the answer to his quests he embraced the true faith. After his acceptance, he delivered a lecture on the 26th August 1904, at the historic Fateh Maidan in Hyderabad. That same year Luzac & Sons printed this lecture, one copy of which is still extant in the British Museum in London. It was later reprinted in 1971 from a copy found by Mr Hasanuddin Ahmad of Hyderabad in the library of Mirza Abul Fazl, also of Hyderabad.

Dr. Nishikant Chattopadhyaye was principal of Hyderabad College and Professor of History at the Maharaja College, Mysore. He was born in mid-nineteenth century in Bengal and died in the first quarter of the 20th century in Hyderabad. His Muslim name after conversion was Mohd Azizuddin.

give you a short sketch of the various phases of doubt and faith through which I have passed from my boyhood upwards to the present day.

Having early lost faith in that strange and heterogeneous medley of animism, fetishism, polytheism and pantheism, known as popular Hinduism, I have been in search of a truer faith from my very boyhood. Naturally enough, I soon came in contact with the Brahmo Somaj and Christianity, then engaged in an apparently bitter conflict for obtaining mastery over the minds of the young Bengal. The star of Babu Keshab Chandra Sen was in the ascendant, and I still recollect the thrill of fervour and enthusiasm with which I used to pour over some of his eloquent sermons and discourses. The Brahmo Somaj introduced me to some of the great Unitarians of England and of America, notably to Theodore Parker of Boston, whom I began to regard as a prophet and an apostle of God. I became so exceedingly fond of his works that it was my habit in those days always to carry a volume or two of Theodore Parker's books with me wherever I happened to go, and to quietly read them over as others do the Bible or the Quran. In this state of mind, I shipped myself off to Europe for the sake of my education. Arrived in Scotland, I soon got into the society of some good Christian men and women of an orthodox type, who began to take great interest in me, and to express great concern for the salvation of my soul. I used to visit their houses and join in their prayer-meetings. Once or twice I even attended some of the revivalistic meetings then in vogue, and was greatly surprised to see strong, bearded men bitterly weeping for their sins, while scores of delicately-framed old spinsters were carried away in fainting fits. The emotional side of the Scotch character of which we see so little in India, now stood revealed before me in a most unequivocal manner. But however deep and genuine my love and reverence for Christ was, however sincere my admiration for the general drift of his essential teachings, I could by no means reconcile myself to two items of the orthodox creed: (1) Atonement, and (2) Eternal Damnation. There was also a Unitarian chapel in Edinburgh that I occasionally attended, and though their religious views and mine were very similar in some respects, yet the general tone of the sermons delivered there was somewhat too cold and sometimes too rationalistic for my warm, oriental blood. In Edinburgh, I fell in with the writings of Thomas Carlyle, who inspired me not only with a genuine love for German literature but also with a real admiration for Luther, Goethe and Schiller. I began to study German in right earnest, and quietly made up my mind to visit that great country which had produced such a grand literature and given birth to such truly heroic souls as mentioned above. The east winds of Edinburgh which ill-suited my naturally delicate constitution, gave me a further plea, and I soon transhipped myself over to Leipzig with a determination to study science, literature and philosophy in the academic halls of that world-renowned University where Lessing and Goethe had finished their studies a century ago. As I was interested in biology and was soon greatly attracted by the Darwinian Theory of Evolution, which was then creating a tremendous ferment all over the German Fatherland, I soon read most of the writings of Buchner and Hackel, of Darwin and of Huxley and above all, of Herbert Spencer. Herbert Spencer had made a practical application of the Evolution Theory to religion and politics, art and society; in other words, to all the multifarious branches of human thought and feelings, and had done so with such a rare vigour of intellect and such an exuberant wealth of illustrations, that I began to consider him as the greatest philosopher that the world had ever produced since Plato and Aristotle, and his Evolution Theory in its practical bearings as the Gospel of the future church of mankind. This Theory of Evolution had, after all, solved all difficulties and set all doubts at rest!

Here was an indisputable *terra firma* on which to build the future superstructure of all human thought and speculation! Did it not account for so many things that were otherwise quite mysterious! True: but it left very little room for the existence of an Almighty, all-knowing and all-good, personal God, for the need of prayer, or for the "hypothesis" of a life after Death where men are to be held responsible for their thoughts, words and deeds. In this manner, I became a Positivist of the schools of Auguste Comte and an Agnostic of the school of Huxley, both at the same time, and was in a very suitable frame of mind to intensely enjoy reading books like Strauss's "The Old and the New Faith" and John Stuart Mill's "Three Essays on Religion" and particularly his charming "Autobiography." Studying some of the German philosophers and especially Arthur Schopenhauer, who was then the *philosophe a la mode* in the student circles of Germany, I soon became a convert to Buddhism which, in its earliest scriptures, inculcates a lofty ethical code minus supernatural sanctions, and a Religion of Humanity minus distinctions of caste, creed and country; Halloa! I had after much wandering found the very religion I was in need of quite close to my own native land, since Buddha had chiefly lived and worked at Gaya and Rajagriha which were anciently included in Bengal and are just now situated on the very borders of the same. I got so exceedingly fascinated with the creed of Lord Buddha that I not only read all the books on Buddhism in English and German that I could lay my hands on, but even learnt Pali to be able to translate a portion of the *Milinda Prasana* in vindication of the right meaning of the *Nirvana* as I then conceived it to be. Professor Max Muller's interpretation, which amounted to the same things, was subsequent to mine. Within a short time I was asked by my German friend to deliver a few lectures on Buddhism, which created quite a flutter in all the clerical and orthodox circles of Germany, inasmuch as in comparing my ideal Buddhism with a very orthodox form of Christianity then in vogue, I had given an unquestionably higher place to Buddhism. These two lectures on "Buddhism and Christianity" were printed, read and criticized all over the country and I had even the gratification of seeing one of them (The Second *Karma*) translated into English and published by the Free Thought Society of London then under the high auspices of Charles Bradlaugh and Annie Besant. When after some 12 years I met Mrs. Besant in Hyderabad for the first time, we were both Theosophists. But the *inherent* pessimism of Buddhism did not appeal to me at all and I soon grew tired of it. Every limb of my body and every faculty of my soul was quivering and aching, as it were, for work and enjoyment, and here was a system of philosophy enjoining on me to deny some and to entirely suppress others of the most natural instincts and emotions of my youth and adolescence. There must be something morbid and radically wrong in a system and a creed that goes against our Human Nature.

When I was passing through this phase of my spiritual life, I had to go, in the first place, to Paris and then a year later on to St. Petersburg. In Paris I soon became quite familiar with the French language which I had already begun to study in Leipzig. French opened, altogether, a new world to me. It gave me, so to say, a new soul. I began to study and take delight in the works of Moliere and Racine, Voltaire and Victor Hugo, Renan and Taine. And quite particularly Voltaire, who appeared and still appears to me the greatest literary genious that the world has ever produced. But the works of Voltaire, though they immensely tickled and amused me, served only to make me a more confirmed sceptic than ever. The forty volumes of his *Oeuvres completes* which range over almost all subjects of human thought and feeling had, however, the effect of laughing me, for good, out of my German gaucherie and Buddhistic pessimism. The influence of Renan, though sceptical, was far more ethical and artistic. His "La Vie de Jesus" (Life of Jesus) is one of the best books I have ever read, deeply impressing me with its poetical style and moral earnestness. Renan led me to take an interest in Semitic religions and in Semitic languages. The works of Max Muller, with which I had been very familiar for several years, had already taught me how to study languages and religions from a scientific standpoint. Renan only continued what Max Muller had already begun, and I threw myself, heart and soul, into the comparative study of all the great religions of the world, to wit: Judaism, Zoroastrianism and

Brahaminism on the one hand, and Buddhism, Christianity and Islam on the other. Christianity for some time appeared to me as the culminating point and the true reconciliation of the Semitic and the Aryan; and I might have become a convert to Roman Catholicism some years ago but for the dogmas of papal infallibility, transubstantiation and so on, which my German university education had rendered untenable. Nevertheless, I was greatly impressed by Roman Catholicism on its artistic and archaeological side and I am still of the opinion, that there is no form of Christianity that affords greater consolation or offers a surer haven to a weary soul tossed for years on the tempestuous seas of modern scepticism, than the Church dedicated to St. Peter in Rome. In this frame of mind I returned to India, and was soon confronted with Theosophy as one of the leading movements of the day. When I was in the service of the late Nawab Sir Viqarul Umarah Bahadur, I was once agreeably surprised to receive through the Nawab Saheb himself the following three books as gifts: (1) Arnold's "Light of Asia." (2) Sinnet's "Occult World" and (3) "Esoteric Buddhism." Who the donor actually was, whether a Tibetan Mahatma or a friendly English book-seller, whence the books really came, whether from the monastries of Lhasa or from the bookstalls of London I have not yet been able to discover, but the books were very useful and interesting reading for some months to come. I soon came in contact with some of the leading apostles of Theosophy and read all their books and pamphlets with great zeal. Theosophy soon revived my old interest in the comparative study of religion, and I now threw myself with special earnestness into the study of Islam and of Zoroastrianism which I had somewhat neglected before. My studies in the old Parsee religion culminated in a lecture on "Zoroastrianism" which was so well appreciated by those for whom it had been intended, that it was printed in a nice pamphlet form under the auspices of the Parsee Panchyat of Bombay. My Islamic studies, for which besides the particular environment of Hyderabad, I had ample resources placed at my disposal in the library of the late Maulvi Cheragh Ali, and that of Mr Syed Ali Bilgrami now in England, brought me into contact with a religion so simple and intelligible, so reasonable and practical, that I should have taken the step I have lately taken some 10 years ago, had not an untoward incident forced me to publish a contradiction in the public journals and to leave Hyderabad altogether for some years. But it was evidently not in the counsels of that all-wise and all-merciful Providence who guides and controls everything, that I should have made this public profession of Islam earlier than I have done. Otherwise I should certainly have done so: He whom Allah guides is rightly guided; but he whom He leaves in error shall find no friend to guide him. (18:17) However, it is better late than never. God is my witness, I have accepted Islam in all sincerity and earnestness, and the first reason that has moved me to do so *is its solid, historical groundwork.* After wandering helplessly for several years in the marshy bogs of divergent creeds and conflicting systems of philosophy, with only the will-o-the-wisp of speculative reason to serve me as a guide, my weary soul has at last found refuge and consolation in a religion based on a Revelation that has remained unaltered ever since its first compilation under the first Caliph, and in a creed that acknowledges as its Prophet of God, one whose historical personality is not only unquestionable but about whose youth, appearance, daily habits and even personal characteristics we know almost as much as we do about those of Oliver Cromwell or of Napoleon Bonaparte. You may slander or revile him if you choose, as so many Christian and other writers have done for centuries, but you can't throw even the least shadow of doubt on the historical basis of that immense personality that has stamped itself so deep on the rolls of Time as to make Christendom grow pale before that august and illustrious name even to this day. But Christendom need not grow pale at all. If it only knew his life and character as it really was—so noble, so genuine and withal, so loveable, Christendom would admire, honour and love him as all Muslims do. In the Prophet Muhammad ﷺ there is nothing vague and shadowy, mythical or mysterious, as, for instance, in Zoroaster and Sreekrishna, or even in Buddha and Christ. The very existence of those Prophets has been seriously doubted and even totally denied; but nobody, as far as I am aware, has ever ventured to reduce the Prophet Muhammad ﷺ either into a "Solar Myth" or into a "fairy tale" as some eminent savants of Europe have done with Buddha and Christ. Oh! What a relief to find, after all, a truly historical Prophet to believe in!

As for the Quran, it is not a mere heterogeneous compilation of a wilderness of stories and chronicles, of Prophetic rhapsodies and of poetical biographies, produced at widely different periods and by widely divergent men, and thrown into one single mould nobody exactly knows when and how; but it is, on the contrary, one single Book bearing the indelible impress of one great Soul to whom

God in His mercy has chosen to reveal it. There is such a marvelous continuity and uniformity running throughout the whole Book, that no impartial critic or fair-minded reader can ever doubt either its sincerity or authenticity. You may call it tedious or monotonous, if you like, you may even point out some of its apparent discrepancies, but you cannot deny its being exactly the same book as that which was revealed to the Holy Prophet during his life-time at different periods and on different occasions ever since that memorable night of the 27th Ramadan (*Lailatul Qadr*) when the angel Gabriel stood before him and said:

> Read, in the name of your Lord, who created, created man from clots of congealed blood. Read! Your Lord is the Most Bountiful One, Who taught man by the Pen, Who taught man what he knew not! Indeed, man transgresses in thinking himself self-sufficient. Verily to your Lord is the return. (96: 1-8)

This historical groundwork of Islam has struck even such a sceptic as Ernst Renan who in his "Etudes d'Histoire Religieu" (pp. 220, 230) makes some very pertinent remarks about it. Professor Bosworth Smith holds similar views and expresses himself in the following terms in his famous lectures on "Muhammad and Islam." "We know indeed, some fragments of a fragment of Christ's life; but who can lift the veil of thirty years that prepared the way for the three? ... But in Islam everything is different; here, instead of the shadowy and the mysterious, we have history. We know as much of Muhammad as we do even of Luther and Milton. The mythical, the legendary, the supernatural is almost wanting in the original Arab authorities, or at all events, can easily be distinguished from what is historical.

Nobody here is the dupe of himself, or of others; there is the full light of day upon all that light can ever reach at all...... In the Quran, we have beyond all reasonable doubt the exact words of Muhammad without subtraction and without addition. We see with our own eyes the birth and adolescence of a religion." (pp. 17, 18, 22) And the last but not the least, Carlyle in his famous book: "Heroes and Hero Worship" has stated the following about the Quran: "When once you get this Quran fairly off, the essential type of it begins to disclose itself: and in this there is merit quite other than the literary one. If a book came from the heart, it will contrive to reach the hearts: all art and authorcraft are of small amount to that. One would say, the primary character of the Quran is that of its genuineness, of its being a bona-fide book. Sincerity in all senses seems to me the merit of the Quran."

The next reason that has induced me to accept Islam is, that it is so eminently reasonable. In Islam, we haven't got to believe in Thirty-nine Articles bristling with dogmas that are either unintelligible to our ordinary reason or inconsistent with our common sense. All that we have to do, is to declare our sincere faith in one simple formula called *kalima: La ilaha illallah, Muhammudur rasullullah*, that is to say, "There is no diety save Allah, and Muhammad is His Prophet." Nay, there is a well-known *Hadith* which distinctly says that even "he who believes only in one God will go to heaven," or in other words is a Muslim *(Man Qala la ilaha illallah fa dakhalal jannah!)*. And is there any human being, from the poorest beggar to the most highly exalted Prince, from the most ignorant poor to the most highly cultured philosopher, who can refuse his sincere adherence to the Unity of God? Every sound and normal man with his human institutions not perverted either by false philosophy or gross depravity, every man, I say, who is not a hopeless atheist or an inveterate agnostic, must readily give his assent to that simple and sublime truth: The Unity of God. All the greatest philosophers of ancient as well as modern times have enunciated it in some shape or other, while saints, apostles and prophets, whose names are so deeply enshrined in the sacred altars of collective humanity, have lived and died for it. What is the verdict of our modern Science on the Unity of Being?, that is to say, the Unity of both force and of matter which compose that Being. Dr. J.C. Bose's recent researches have only scientifically demonstrated what apostles and prophets have invariably and persistently proclaimed ever since the days of Adam and Noah, Abraham and Moses. In Islam, we are not asked to believe in three gods—in One as in the Athanasian creed, or in thirty millions of gods and goddesses as in popular Hinduism, but only in that one great Being who is the Creator of the Universe, who is all-knowing and all-wise and who is, at the same time, also the most merciful and the most compassionate: "Your God is one God; there is no God but He, the Most Merciful. In the creation of the Heavens and Earth, and the alternation of night and day, and in the ships that sail the ocean, laden with what is profitable to mankind, and in the rain and the water which God sends from Heaven, quickening again dead earth, and the animals of all sorts which cover its surface, and in the movements of winds and the clouds balanced between heaven and earth are signs to people of understanding; Yet there are some who worship other objects besides Allah, bestowing on them the adoration due to Allah." (2: 164-65).

As to the second part of the *kalima*, it is not a "necessary fiction" as Gibbon chooses to call it, but a very necessary and highly valuable truth consistent with reason, and appealing to the highest aspirations of our spiritual life. Whenever the fundamental truths, on which our moral and religious life is based, are either obscured or forgotten, whenever men become too worldly and avaricious, too immoral and materialistic, there appear, in the history of races and nations, men so highly spiritualised by birth and breeding as to be called prophets and apostles of God, and whose sole mission in life is to remind men of what they have forgotten and to revive what they have lost. "I am no more than a public preacher. I preach nothing new. I only try to bring home to you certain eternal truths proclaimed by all true prophets of God which you have evidently forgotten." This is being constantly repeated in the Quran. And that the Prophet Muhammad ﷺ was all that he claimed to be, namely a Prophet of God in the highest sense of that word, will be evident to all fair-minded men, unbiased by missionary or sectarian prejudices, who take the trouble to study his life and teachings and particularly the Quran which has been called the "autobiography of Muhammad." All the Traditions represent him as uncommonly true and just, liberal and generous, good and pure. He has been the beau ideal of a Perfect Man to one-third of our race for the last 13 centuries. It is absurd to suppose, that "a wicked impostor" as Christian writers commonly represent him to be, should have had that immense and abiding influence on such vast masses of men for such a long time as Muhammad. After all, Carlyle's dictum, contained in his lecture on "Heroes and Hero-worship" which I have already referred to, will be found to be true:

"This deep-hearted son of the wilderness with his beaming black eyes, and open, social, deep soul had other thoughts in him than ambition. A silent, great soul, he was one of those who cannot but be in earnest; whom nature herself has appointed to be sincere. While others work in formulas and hearsays, contented enough to dwell therein, this man could not screen himself in formulas: he was alone with his whole soul and the reality of things. The great mystery of existence glared upon him with its terrors, with its splendours; no hearsays could hide that unspeakable fact, 'Here am I.' Such sincerity as we named it has, in truth, something of the divine. The word of such a man is a voice direct from nature's own heart. Men must listen to that, or to nothing else; all else is wind in comparison. From of old, a thousand thoughts in his pilgrimages and wanderings had been in this man 'What am I ?' 'What is Life?' 'What is Death?' 'What am I to believe?' 'What am I to do?' The grim rocks of Mount Hira, or Mount Sinai, the stern, sandy solitude answered not. The great Heaven rolling silently overhead with its blue glancing stars, answered not. There was no answer. The man's own soul and what of God's inspirations dwelt there, had to answer!"

These two fundamental principles, whose profession makes a man a Muslim, are thus based on the highest dictates of our intuitive reason. This has been admitted even by Christian writers such as Edward Montet who, in his book called *"La propaganda chretienne et ses adversaires Mussalmans"* has written the following: "Islam is a religion that is essentially rationalistic in the widest sense of this term, considered etymologically and historically. The definition of rationalism as a system that bases religious beliefs on principles furnished by the reason, applies to it exactly. To believers, the Muslim creed is summed up in belief in the Unity of God and in the mission of His Prophet, statements that, to the religious man rest on the firm basis of reason. This fidelity to the fundamental dogma of the religion that has been proclaimed with a grandeur, majesty, and an invariable purity and with a note of sure conviction which it is hard to find surpassed outside the pale of Islam, the elemental simplicity of the formula in which it is enunciated, the proof that it gains from the fervid conviction of the missionaries who propagate it, are so many causes to explain the success of Muslim missionary efforts. A creed so precise, so stripped of all theological complexities and, consequently, so accessible to the ordinary understanding, might be expected to possess and does indeed possess a marvellous power of winning its way into the consciences of men." (pp. 17-18)

The third reason why I have accepted Islam is, that it is so thoroughly practical. Its ethical code is based on the actual needs of human nature, and not on some imaginary or exaggerated standard of virtue which is unattainable. The standard set up by other religions, for example, by Buddhism and Christianity might, in a certain sense, be called loftier or more transcendental; but is it possible to realise it in actual life? The test by which an ethical code is to be judged is not its poetical beauty, but its practical utility, by its complete adaptation to the needs and requirements of our human nature as it is. As Emerson has beautifully put it: "Sirius may be loftier than the Sun, but it does not ripen my grapes!" We may admire Quixotic perfections in novels and romances, but they are utterly useless in the struggles of our everyday life. We may admire, for example, the poetic excellence of the precept: "When thy brother smites thee on thy right cheek, turn to him the left also," but does any Christian, good, bad or indifferent, ever practise it? Take again the doctrines of celibacy and marriage. Both Buddhism and Christianity, though they tolerate marriage, yet exalt celibacy as a higher virtue. Islam does not tolerate celibacy at all, but, on the contrary, enjoins matrimony as a religious duty binding on every true Muslim.

This system of universal matrimony, joined to occasional polygamy amongst the wealthier classes, makes it, that there is almost a total dearth in Muslim countries of those professional out-castes such as you invariably come across in such shockingly large figures in the streets of London and Paris, Vienna and St. Petersburg. Canon Isaac Taylor, a dignitary of the Anglican Church , had the courage to deliver himself in the following manner before a Church Congress held at Wolverhampton on the 7th October 1887: "Muhammad limited the unbounded license of polygamy; it is the exception rather than the rule in the most civilized Muslim lands—European Turkey, Algiers and Egypt. Polygamy, with all its evils, has its counterbalancing advantages. It has abolished female infanticide and gives every woman a legal protector. Owing to polygamy, Muslim countries are free from professional outcasts, a greater reproach to Christendom than polygamy to Islam. The strictly regulated polygamy of the Muslim is infinitely less degrading to women and less injurious to men than the promiscuous polyandry which is the course of Christian cities and which is absolutely unknown in Islam. The polyandrous English are not entitled to cast stones at polygamous Muslims. Let us first pluck out the beam from our own eye, before we meddle with the mote in our brother's eye." Now, which matrimonal code, do you think, is more practical, more consonant to the actual needs of human society and more conducive to its highest development from a moral and spiritual point of view? I could bring forward other moral precepts of Islam and, contrasting them with those of other great religions of the world, point out how in each case there is in Islam a far more harmonious blending of practical wisdom and spiritual insight than anywhere else. But that would lead me too far and demand a separate lecture by itself. For this occasion I shall only content myself by quoting the following passage from Amir Ali's famous book, *The Spirit of Islam:* "The practical character of a religion, its abiding influence on the common relations of mankind, in the affairs of every-day life, its power on masses, are the true criteria for judging of its universality.....In Islam is joined a lofty idealism with the most rationalistic practicality. It did not ignore human nature, it never entangled itself in the tortuous pathways which lie outside the domain of the actual and the real. Its object, like that of other systems, was the elevation of humanity towards the absolute ideal of perfection, but it attained or tries to attain this object by grasping the truth, that the nature of man is, in this existence, imperfect." (p. 278).

These are some of the chief reasons, practical and speculative, that have induced me to accept Islam in preference to the other great religions of the world. There are also the reasons which have always appealed strongly in favour of Islam to some of the greatest minds of Europe in the past as well as in the present. It would be quite out of place here to allude even en passant to what Voltaire, Goethe, Gibbon in the 18th, and a host of great men in the 19th century have said about Islam. All that is possible to do in a lecture like this is to make a passing allusion to a few Europeans of the present day, who have expressed their sympathy and admiration for the faith of Islam.

Not long ago, we all read of a distinguished English nobleman (Lord Stanley of Alderley) who is reputed to have declared before his death that he had all his life been a Muslim! I can assure you, that there are hundreds and thousand all over Europe and America, who would do exactly the same, if they had the requisite moral courage to brave the social and other disadvantages attending on such a step. It was not less a man and a savant than Ernst Renan who has said the following in his famous lecture on *"L' Islamisme and la science"* (p.19):- *"Je ne suis jamais entré dans une mosquée sans une vive emotion, le dirai-je? sans un certain regret de n'être pas un Mussulman!"* that is to say, "I have never been inside a mosque without feeling a strong emotion, shall I confess it? Without a certain amount of regret that I am not a Muslim"! When a great scholar and great sceptic like Ernst Renan could make a declaration like that, what of humbler persons and individuals—what about the ordinary unlettered people of the world? Since it is well-known that Islam, owing to its simplicity intelligibility and practicality, is specially suited for the masses of mankind and that it is with the masses that it always had its most signal success and achieved its greatest triumphs, the Rev. Marcus Dodd, D.D. in his book on

"Muhammad, Buddha and Christ" has stated the following about the same: "The extreme simplicity of the creed of Islam greatly favoured its rapid propagation. No elaborate explanations were required to teach the ignorant....The rude Negro could understand it on its first recital....It demanded no long novitiate....it was a creed for which the human mind has an instinctive affinity, and which has never roused abhorrence even in the mind of a polytheist. To men who had begun to despair of finding the truth amidst the bewildering subtleties of a metaphysical theology, it was a relief to find themselves face to face with a simple creed and to be compelled to believe it." (pp. 100-7)

Hence, I feel sure, that if a comprehensive Islamic mission were started in Hyderabad (or any other central place) to preach the simple and sublime truths of Islam to the people of Europe, America and Japan, there would be such a rapid and enormous accession to its ranks as had not been witnessed again ever since the first centuries of the Hijra. You all know the good work which Abdulla W.H. Quilliam has been doing for several years in Liverpool. Besides winning actual converts whose number runs up to some two hundred in all, he has rendered valuable service to the Muslim world by his books and pamphlets which have dissipated prejudices and awakened a lively interest in Islam all over the civilised world. Some of his pamphlets are widely read all over India and Burma, and have, I believe, been translated into Burmese, Hindustani, Persian and Arabic. Don't you feel that it is your bounden duty to stengthen his hands as much you are able to do, and to help him to disseminate the faith of Islam in Europe as he has been doing with such signal success for so many years? Will you, therefore, organise a grand central Islamic Mission here in Hyderabad and open branches in Europe, America and in Japan? God's choicest blessings will descend on Hyderabad, and especially on the Head of its beloved and beneficent Ruler: Mir Mahboob Ali Khan, His Highness the Nizam of Hyderabad!

It has been well said, that our choice even in the most exalted matters often proceeds from mixed motives. Shall I tell you what further subconscious motive or reason has had its influence in deciding my choice of Islam? It is this: *To consecrate for the remainder of my earthly days what gifts God has given me and what knowledge and capacity I have acquired, either in Europe or in Asia, from books as well as from travels, to the service of that great community to which I have now the privilege to belong.* Will you then accept me as a brother, as a friend and as a servant? Allow me now to finish this lecture of mine that has already taxed your patience longer than I had intended, with the following verse from the Holy Quran:

> Say: "My Lord has guided me to a straight path, to an upright religion, to the faith of the upright Abraham; for he was not one of those who join gods with God. Say: Verily, my prayers, and my worship, and my life and my death are unto God, Lord of the Worlds. He has no associate, and this I am commanded; and I am the first of those who submit to His will." (6: 161-162)

25

❦

Conclusion

The nineteenth century was the century of theknowledge explosion. Man came to feel that, under the influence of science, the attainment of boundless knowledge was within his reach, and that he was now in a position to build his world on his own. However, by the end of this century the picture was quite different. It was discovered with great frustration that science can give but a partial knowledge of reality. And limited knowledge is an insufficient basis on which to construct an ideology that will provide answers to all his questions. The first phase of—hope—was outlined in a book written by the British author, Julian Huxley: *Man Stands Alone*. The second phase of–frustration–found expression in a book written by the American author, Cressy Morrison. Its title: *Man does Not Stand Alone* was truly meaningful.

But again there was the thrilling news brought by the twentieth century: that of the atomic explosion. Man believed once again that he had managed to acquire the greatest power of nature; now the time had come for the first time in human history to build the most successful civilization on earth.

Events showed, however, that atomic power, having assumed the form of the atomic bomb, became a source of such great destruction as to threaten the very existence of human civilization.

The truth is that prior to the knowledge explosion, or the atomic explosion, man has been in need of a reliable ideology to furnish him with a complete interpretation of life, and instruct him as to the goal of his existence and the direction of his actions and how to exercise knowledge and power. The spread of communism in the nineteenth century had given man the false conviction that he had discovered the perfect ideology that he had been seeking all along. But, in 1991, with the collapse of the Soviet Union, this false sense of conviction vanished into thin air. In this new scenario, the world is experiencing an ideological vacuum. Islam alone can fill this vacuum for it is a religion of nature—a complete and preserved guidebook handed down by God to His Prophet.

The trend of studying Islam all over the world shows that this process has already begun and the twenty first century will be the century of Islam. If the nineteenth century was marked by the knowledge explosion and the twentieth century by the atomic explosion, the twenty first century is destined to be marked by the Islamic explosion.

The fact is that, for the building of life, man is in need of divine guidance. Religion is the name of this divine guidance. And Islam is the only preserved and reliable version of religion. Just as there is no source of physical light save that of the sun, similarly there is no other source of divine guidance for life except that of Islam. Islam is the only reliable, authentic and dependable answer to this question.

Man, born to live on the planet earth, has been endowed with free choice, but he is not the master of his destiny. The most crucial aspect of life is that he is accountable to God Almighty for all his deeds. There is no escape from this accountability. After a brief span on earth, he is destined to face his death and find himself before God for his fate to be decided in the form of eternal hell or eternal paradise. The greatest of man's concerns is that he should prepare himself for the world to come. The present world is like a great examination hall, where man's only task is to pass the divine test set by God, so that he may save himself from divine punishment in the next world, and be held deserving of God's rewards in the form of paradise. In paradise there will be no fear and no regret.

Everyone is heading towards a fateful leap into the next world. Only those who can pass the divine test are the successful ones in this life and the next. This is the goal towards which people ought to strive. (Qur'an 37:60).

Tell Me About HAJJ

What the Hajj Is, Why It's So Important and What It Teaches Me

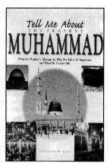

Tell Me About MUHAMMAD

What the Prophet's Message Is, Why His Life is So Important and What He Teaches Me

Tell Me About THE PROPHET MUSA

What the Prophet's Message Is, Why His Life is So Important and What He Teaches Me

THE MIRACLE IN THE ANT

HARUN YAHYA

ALLAH IS KNOWN THROUGH REASON

HARUN YAHYA

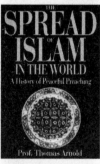

Children's Stories from the Quran
The Origin of Life
Colouring Book

LIFE BEGINS
Quran Stories for Little Hearts

THE SPREAD OF ISLAM IN THE WORLD
A History of Peaceful Preaching

Prof. Thomas Arnold

Islamic Medicine

EDWARD G. BROWNE

Islamic Thought and Its Place in History

De Lacy O'Leary

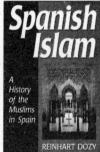

ISLAM REDISCOVERED
Discovering Islam from its Original Sources

MAULANA WAHIDUDDIN KHAN

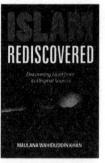

THE ISLAMIC ART AND ARCHITECTURE

SIR THOMAS ARNOLD

DECISIVE MOMENTS IN THE HISTORY OF ISLAM

MUHAMMAD ABDULLAH ENAN

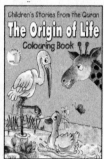

A HAND BOOK OF MUSLIM BELIEF

DR. AHMAD A. GALWASH

Spanish Islam
A History of the Muslims in Spain

REINHART DOZY